KT-451-784

Nanny Pat

Queen of the Rising Sun

From Landlady of an East End Pub to Essex Nan

PAN BOOKS

First published 2013 by Pan Books
an imprint of Pan Macmillan, a division of Macmillan Publishers Limited
Pan Macmillan, 20 New Wharf Road, London N1 9RR
Basingstoke and Oxford
Associated companies throughout the world
www.panmacmillan.com

ISBN 978-1-4472-1878-4

Copyright © Patricia Brooker and Emma Donnan 2013

The right of Patricia Brooker and Emma Donnan to be identified as the
authors of this work has been asserted by them in accordance
with the Copyright, Designs and Patents Act 1988.

The picture acknowledgements on page 302
constitute an extension of this copyright page.

All rights reserved. No part of this publication may be
reproduced, stored in or introduced into a retrieval system, or
transmitted, in any form, or by any means (electronic, mechanical,
photocopying, recording or otherwise) without the prior written
permission of the publisher. Any person who does any unauthorized
act in relation to this publication may be liable to criminal
prosecution and civil claims for damages.

1 3 5 7 9 8 6 4 2

A CIP catalogue record for this book is available from
the British Library.

Map by HL Studios, Witney, Oxon
Typeset by Ellipsis Digital Limited, Glasgow
Printed and bound by CPI Group (UK) Ltd, Croydon CR0 4YY

This book is sold subject to the condition that it shall not,
by way of trade or otherwise, be lent, re-sold, hired out,
or otherwise circulated without the publisher's prior consent
in any form of binding or cover other than that in which
it is published and without a similar condition including this
condition being imposed on the subsequent purchaser.

Visit **www.panmacmillan.com** to read more about all our books
and to buy them. You will also find features, author interviews and
news of any author events, and you can sign up for e-newsletters
so that you're always first to hear about our new releases.

To Charlie

TOWER HAMLETS LIBRARIES	
91000001885821	
Bertrams	14/02/2013
BIO791.45	£7.99
THISBO	TH12002556

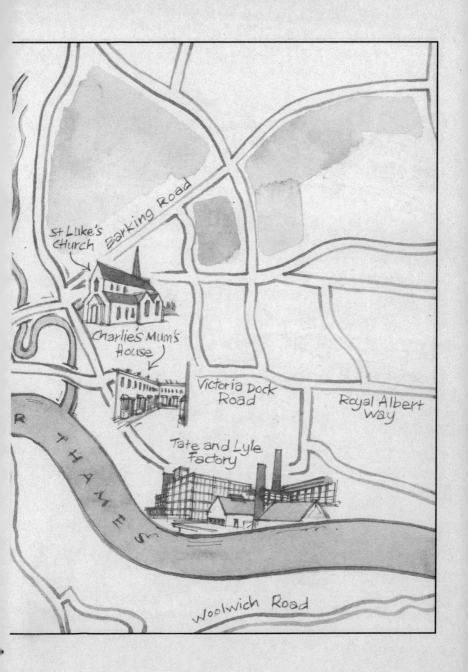

CONTENTS

PROLOGUE

Try to imagine the most unlikely pub landlady you can. Go on, what are the worst qualities she could have? Perhaps someone quiet and shy, who is innocent and easily shocked. Who likes to spend time with close family rather than strangers sitting at the bar. And, of course, someone who doesn't drink. Not exactly traits you would look for in a woman running a bar – and especially not an East End pub!

I'm not talking about the East End of London of today, however, with its glamorous Olympic Park and visitors arriving from all around the world. No, I'm talking about the East End of the 1960s. Where the buildings that attracted the most punters were the pubs – now knocked down to make way for the Olympic development – and the most exotic visitors were from the next borough over. Back then a landlady was expected to be

1

particularly lively, tough, and at the centre of all the action.

But I hold my hands up – the description at the top of the page is the thirty-two-year-old me to a tee. Yet there I was in 1968, standing behind a bar, shaking like a leaf, and about to attempt a job I had never imagined myself doing.

No, it was not my idea. It was my husband Charlie's. And despite the fact that we had five young children, aged between four and eleven, he thought it would be a doddle, running the pub and bringing 'em up. Oh, those were the days . . .

In my first book, *Penny Sweets And Cobbled Streets*, I told you the story of my childhood – growing up in the East End in the forties and fifties, being evacuated in the war and learning to run the household from the age of eleven after my mum died. I talked about being a young woman working in the factories, meeting Charlie, setting up home with him and starting our family.

But although those were eventful times, that was only the start of it all. This part of my story is where the adventure really begins. There have been happy times and sad times, and we never knew what was round the corner. I may not have expected to find myself behind a bar in my thirties, but I *definitely* didn't expect to become a TV star in my seventies!

It's these memories that I'm going to share with you now. And I hope that by telling my story I can bring to life just how much things have changed over the past fifty years – not just for the East End and Essex, but for little ol' me too!

ONE

Life as an East End Landlady

So there I was, in January 1968, about to begin life as an East End pub landlady and, as I say, probably the most unlikely character around to be doing the job. I had never set foot in a pub before then, if you can believe it, as in them days pubs were not seen as a place for women. So you'll understand why I kept thinking to myself, 'What the bleedin' hell is Charlie thinking buying us a pub to run?!'

But my husband was so upbeat about it, so sure we were doing the right thing, and I could see it was a real dream of his. So I decided I was going to be positive about it and get stuck into it with as much enthusiasm as I could. And so my life as a landlady began.

The Rising Sun pub was at 199 St Leonard's Street in Bromley-by-Bow. It was a nice-looking, quite new red-brick building. At the time the area was very working-class, with not a lot of money but tons of character and community spirit – very similar to where I had been brought up, just round the corner in nearby Devons Road.

The Rising Sun was in a group of four pubs. We were on one side of the road, with another pub, The Duke of Wellington, a bit further along. Then across from us was The Aberfelde – so called as it was on the corner of Aberfelde Road – and a fourth one, whose name I can't for the life of me remember. Together they acted as the four locals for everyone who lived and worked nearby.

Just down from us was a row of shops, including a greengrocer's, a sweet shop and a tobacconist. Everything the locals needed really. There was also a fire station, and there were plenty of flats roundabouts, meaning lots of locals and potential drinkers! Sadly all the pubs and the shops have since gone – there is literally nothing left of it all now. First they were redeveloped and these huge great buildings appeared – office blocks or something, I think they were. Now a lot of the area is changed because of the Olympics. I'm sure it is all very nice, but it certainly doesn't have the character it did back then.

But anyway, it is back then I am really concerned with, and us about to open our pub . . . with no experience!

The Rising Sun had originally been one of my husband Charlie's local drinking places of an evening, and when the landlady was selling up and she mentioned it to him, thinking it would be his kind of thing, he decided to buy the lease. He had never run a pub before, but my Charlie was a bit of a Jack of all trades – he could turn his hand to all sorts of jobs, and had done so in our time together. 'A bit of this and that' was the East End way. He had served in the army and the navy, been a handyman for the council, worked on the docks maintaining the boats, helped out in the cellars of a few of the local pubs . . . anything that helped him get the money in. So when the landlady made her suggestion, the idea took hold and that was it. We packed up from our home in Bray Drive, Canning Town, where we had lived since we got married thirteen years before, and made our way over to Bromley-by-Bow.

There was no time to get into things slowly and learn the way of the trade before we opened. Oh no. We only had one day to settle in before we opened for business! Charlie didn't want people thinking the pub had closed in case they had time to find themselves a new local, and the previous landlady had left us some stock as part of the deal, so that was it, we opened.

I had got my three girls off to school first thing in the morning – June, the eldest at eleven, was at a secondary school along Roman Road, which was just a few minutes away so she walked there herself; then Susan, eight, and Carol, seven, were at a local primary school which, luckily for us, was just round the corner from The Rising Sun, so it took me no time at all to get them down there. And then there were my two boys Stephen, five, and the baby of the family, Little Charlie, who was four, whom I had left upstairs playing.

It was 11.30 a.m. and I was standing behind the bar, as nervous as anything, when Charlie opened the doors. I remember I was wearing my best cotton dress, a cream one with little flowers all over it. There were no uniforms or anything in our pub, but it was never trousers for me – always just a nice dress. We didn't want it too formal in there like. Just somewhere people felt at home.

There were actually two rooms to the bar in the beginning. There was the main section, where you got all the men coming in for their pints, and then a smaller room called the snug. That was where you went if you wanted a quieter, private drink, and where kids were allowed if they were waiting for their dads. A bit like me in the old days, when I would go down to my dad's local with him, but they at least got to set foot a bit further through the door – I had to wait outside!

The snug was also where we had what was called the off-licence – where you went if you wanted a pint to take away with you, to drink in the peace of your own home. It was what the older generation of women enjoyed doing, such as my nan, Ol' Polly Spicer, when she was alive.

In the main bar, we had stools running along the length of it, and then a few tables and chairs dotted around the room. There was an old fireplace and the whole room had quite a homely, welcoming feel to it. I can't remember the exact décor, but it was all quite dark, dull colours – you didn't go in for bright, garish colours in them days – and it had nice wooden floors. It smelt of beer and smoke – a strange mix for me at first, but I got used to it after a while and ended up quite liking it as it was so familiar.

There was a darts board and a set of darts, although no pool tables or anything like that – I don't think any pubs back then really went in for that. Then behind the bar we had all the usual drinks on sale. We had a couple of taps of bitters and beers from the brewery, Watney Mann, who owned the pub, although nothing like the selection you get today. Most of the beers, including the light and dark ales and Guinness, were in bottles in the fridge, and so were the little bottles of soft drinks like lemonade.

On the back counter we had the spirits. We used to hang up some, such as whisky and gin, on one of these two round rotating stands at each end of the bar, with optics. The optics were given to us by the brewery and were new at the time in pubs. They were great as they saved us having to work out the amount ourselves – you just pushed the glass up into 'em to get a measure. And then there were others just standing on the counter, which you had to measure out in a little gold cup before pouring it into a glass – measures then were the same as today, 25 ml.

So there was good choice of drinks, but not everything what they have these days. There weren't wines, and we didn't do cocktails or all that business.

We also sold packets of cigarettes and crisps. There were just the two flavours – salted or cheese and onion. None of all the fancy ones you can get today! They were Smith's crisps and you made the salted ones yourself. The crisps would be unsalted, but there was a blue square packet of salt in the bag that you'd tear open and sprinkle over the crisps, then you'd shake up the packet and they'd be ready to eat.

Arrowroot biscuits were still really popular too, just like the ones my dad used to give me as a child to distract me while I waited for him as he drank in the pub. They cost a penny and were these big digestive-type biscuits that everyone who grew up in the East End at that time would remember. I think you can still get some sort of a version of 'em nowadays, but they are smaller and not really the same. Which is probably no bad thing – looking back I've no idea why we loved them as they tasted a bit like cardboard, I reckon it's only dogs what might get fed the original ones these days!

I can't remember the first person who came into the bar the first day we opened, but I do remember that I didn't serve or speak to 'em 'cause of how terrified I was. I left it to Charlie to serve the punters until it got busy and I had no choice but to join in. Oh and in the end I was rightly run off my feet, and panicking trying to work it all out. I hadn't got a clue what half the drinks were that people were ordering, and was spilling them all over the place; my hands were shaking so much with nerves. I kept looking helplessly at Charlie, who just laughed at me and then showed me what to do. My God, I had to learn quick, 'cause you just had to get on with it and make it work.

And it's not like they even kept it simple, just going for a pint of the ale or bitter we had on tap. No, it was things like 'a pint of light and dark, love'. Well what the bleedin' hell was that?! I didn't know. But turned out it was light ale and brown ale, half and half, mixed together. That was a popular one, and cost one shilling and eleven pence a pint, if I remember right – about ten pence in today's money. Cheap the drinks were then. I'll tell you what, you could get a few people drunk on a fiver – not like today when one drink is a fiver!

Then there was the till. We had one of those ones where you had to key in the amount for each drink then total it up yourself – the till didn't do the maths for you – but I couldn't understand the bleedin' thing that first day! So I was all like scribbling numbers down on a piece of paper with a pencil I had by the till and reckoning things up that way, and then saying to myself, 'Right, don't forget that, and then add that up . . .', all the while scurrying around like a blue-arsed fly.

And in between all the serving, I was forever running up and down the stairs to check on the boys. They were still so young that I felt guilty leaving them on their own, but there was nothing else I could do so I just made sure to check on 'em a lot. Although it was exhausting – there were about thirty very steep stairs to get to the upper floor!

I didn't even feel like I had time to stop and look at the customers and work out whether we were doing all right. I suppose you could say it was just about surviving that first lunchtime rather than anything else.

But Charlie was in his element and was the perfect publican. Oh, while I was all in a fluster and busily counting on my fingers, rushing around with my head down, he was chatting away and making new friends with just about everyone who came in there. And they all seemed to like him – who wouldn't? He was a big cheerful chatty man, with a cheeky smile and a twinkle in his eye. He was sharp too and had a great sense of humour. But he was tough and respected as well. All the characteristics people like in a landlord.

I was exhausted when the lunchtime shift ended, but in a strange sort of way I think I had enjoyed it, in between all the stressful moments. It was a challenge anyhow, and I had decided to give it a go, so giving it a good go I was!

And of course there was no sitting and relaxing after the lunchtime shift was over and we closed the doors at 2 p.m. No. I had to go and collect the kids from school and make them some dinner, before heading out the door to do an evening shift at Tate & Lyle. Because, yes, I was still working over at the sugar factory on Factory Road in Silvertown.

So just as Charlie was getting the pub ready for the evening session, which started at 5.30 p.m., I was rushing out the door to get over to Tate & Lyle for a shift lasting from 5 until 9 p.m. Although it was the first time Charlie would be on his own behind the bar, he clearly didn't mind – I could see he was in his element. And, true enough, by the time I got back he was stood at the bar chatting with the locals as though he had been running The Rising Sun for years.

I got out of my factory clothes and pulled my dress back on to help do the last bits of serving, and then Charlie called out 'time' and the last few people in the pub headed on their way. As Charlie shut and locked the door behind them I felt like collapsing with relief. It had seemed like the longest day ever, but somehow we had got through it!

Not that closing the door meant the end of the day. No, then we had to do the accounts and work out all our takings. It was exhausting. Just as my brain wanted to shut down, it was having to do its toughest work of the day. And accounts was something new to me as well, so really I sat and watched Charlie and just did what he told me to do.

I don't remember what our takings were that day, but I know Charlie said to me that it was 'not a bad start. I think this is going to work out!' So we headed off to bed exhausted, but with a sense of satisfaction that we had survived our first day as East End publicans!

And that was it. We got ourselves into a bit of a routine so that each day was pretty similar to the first. It was tiring, though, and I did wonder how long I could keep up my shift at Tate & Lyle too. There it was my job to get cane sugar into bags. I would put the bags under a machine, which would pour out the sugar in either 1 lb or 2 lb amounts, depending on what was needed that day. Then I would pass 'em to the next person, who would stick the packets closed. Other times I had to put the boxes under where the sugar cubes came out and watch out for broken ones. It was an all right job. The bosses were nice enough and there were some entertaining girls working there who kept everyone's spirits up with their chats and songs. But, to be honest, I was just plain tired from the day I'd already done, so by the time I got there, work was the last thing on my mind.

While I was at Tate & Lyle, Charlie kept a bit of an eye on the kids and played with 'em when he had a moment. But luckily my eldest, June, was able to help out too as she was getting on – she was eleven by then. In fact, all the girls were old enough by then to take reasonable care of themselves, and they'd all have a bath together and make sure the little 'uns were clean before bed.

If any of them weren't yet in bed when I got home, I'd get them settled before going down to the bar to help Charlie out with what was left of the evening. If it was Monday to Thursday, we'd close up at 10.30 p.m., but on Fridays and Saturdays it was 11 p.m., and then 10 p.m. on a Sunday.

And counting the money afterwards did start to get easier as the days went by, although it did always leave me with a kind of brain ache! Them days it was pounds, shillings and pence – the old money. And me and Charlie, of course we had to sit there and tally up every ha'penny, penny, shilling, half a crown, two-bob bit . . . everything. It used to take more time reckoning up our money once people had gone home for the night than it did serving when people were there. Oh, it used to be a headache. But you couldn't ignore it or it'd be confusion and double the work the next night. Then once a week Charlie would head off to the bank, to put money in if all had gone well, and deal with anything he needed to do.

The way it worked, is before the start of the shift you would stock up on everything behind the bar and then count it. So say you had twenty bottles of lager, fifteen small lemonade bottles, ten packets of fags, etc. You would write that down on a piece of paper – or I would. If you were Charlie, you would just memorize it. Then at the end of the shift you would count again, and the difference was how many of each item you had sold. If all went to plan, that would tally up with the amount that had gone into the till. And if it didn't, well, we could spend hours counting and recounting until we found the whereabouts of every pound!

Then it was off to bed for a few hours before morning arrived and it was time to get the kids to school and start the whole day again. Oh, I swear, I never stopped!

TWO
The Locals – Good and Bad

After a couple of weeks we had, I suppose, got into a routine, and I was beginning to get to grips with what each drink was and how to work the till. I had started serving food at lunchtime too. Nothing special, mind. Just plates of sandwiches or a filled roll if someone asked for 'em. There was no kitchen downstairs, though, so I had to go upstairs and make them there, before putting them in the dumb waiter and winding them down to Charlie below.

The dumb waiter was this small lift that you operated yourself on a pulley, winding it up and down. It went from the top floor, down to the pub, and then on down to the cellar, so it would help get things from there too. It made life easier than running up and down the stairs with lunch plates anyhow.

The cellar, meantime, was Charlie's territory. You

would get down there by stairs at the back of the pub. It was cold down there, very cold, and dark, although there was a light that we left on permanently. But it was the kind of place where the light didn't really seem to fill the room, if you know what I mean.

I'd go down there sometimes to get drinks, but it was Charlie who changed the barrels and checked the stock when it was delivered by the cellar men, who came from the brewery once a week, I think it was, in their lorry. They would pull up out the front by this other entrance into the cellar. It was like these loft doors that opened up in the ground. Then they'd set up these two planks of wood that ran through the door down to the cellar floor, and one man would roll the barrels down from the top, while the other would be at the bottom waiting to catch them and stack them up. As and when they were needed, Charlie would connect the big metal barrels to taps in the cellar, which then fed through to the pumps up in the bar.

So it was all going smoothly – or as much as we could hope – and everything was falling into place. I was still building up confidence with the customers, though – that was still very much Charlie's territory. The punters were mainly locals who would come in regularly. A lot of them lived in the flats just behind the pub, on the Coventry Cross Estate. This was a council estate just like any other in the area, where everyone was friendly, hard-working, and living as best they could.

They were mostly elderly men, or older than me anyhow, and they would pop in most nights for a few pints before bed. They liked The Rising Sun because it was a friendly, family pub – although without the children, if you know what I mean.

Saturdays were much busier – we could have anywhere between fifty and seventy people in there at a time, maybe more. It would be quite a crowd and we'd be rushed off our feet.

It helped that my dad's older brother Joe lived in Coventry Cross as he helped us out in the early days, encouraging people to come down, introducing them to us and making them – and us – feel right at home. He knew the best part of people in the pub pretty much any night of the week.

Joe was great at that time. He was a painter and decorator like my dad, although they worked separately, and he was a proper East End character. He was a good-looking fella, well built with a shock of ginger hair, a good heart, and a cheeky, happy-go-lucky charm. Me and Charlie were really close to him, as was my dad, of course, and the kids loved him.

Dad came in for a drink of an evening too from time to time and knew a lot of the customers already through

Joe. He and Joe would sit at the bar and hold court, and after they'd had a few, a sing-song might start.

Just as when I was a child watching Dad through the door of his favourite local, Kitsons on Devons Road, right by our flats, I could see he was in his element, and that sitting in a pub was where he felt most at home. It must also have helped that he knew he had lent us some of the money needed for the bar. Because although we paid him back as quickly as we could, I am sure he always felt that he had an interest in The Rising Sun.

My dad had a girlfriend too, Bet Abrahams, who he had been with for about thirteen years, and she would sometimes come with him. He was fifty-six by this time, and, although I never asked, I always had the idea she was a few years older.

My mum was no longer alive – she had died when I was just eleven years old. At the time, as you can imagine, I was absolutely distraught, so I hadn't been that happy when Bet had come on the scene in my teenage years as I felt like no one could replace my mum. But by this stage I had realized that she was good company for Dad, and I had come to accept her. She was a dark haired, fairly ordinary-looking woman, and the two of them understood each other well.

Anyway, mostly these locals would come in on their own, but they all knew each other so would sit up at the bar chatting to each other or talking to us – mainly Charlie, but sometimes me too. And they loved to have a good moan and tell you their problems. I soon discovered that being a landlord or landlady means you are considered a bit of a counsellor as well, although more often than not they didn't want advice, just someone to listen. So I mostly just nodded, and made sympathetic noises!

They rarely opened up to us about serious problems, though – just everyday strife. It wasn't the East End way to start confessing serious money troubles or the likes. People were too proud for that, and that kind of problem stayed private.

Sometimes the complaints would make me laugh. Such as those from Sam, an overweight man of about forty, who would be in most days after his shift in a local factory. He would say things like, 'I'm in trouble with the wife at the minute, as turns out I forgot her birthday last week. You're a woman, Pat. How do I make her start talking to me again?'

The problem was, he seemed to be in trouble with her most weeks for something or other!

Other regulars would sit at a table by themselves, drinking their pints at the end of a day at work, lost in thought in their own little worlds. They seemed to enjoy the time alone, so we mostly left them to it. Mainly, we served the pints in a glass, both normal pint glasses and glass ones with handles. But some of the older regulars still preferred a metal tankard so we had a few of them behind the counter, and each of them belonged to someone, so they'd get their drink in their own jug. Like I say, some of them definitely treated the pub like it was their home!

Over the first few weeks of us taking over The Rising Sun, the couples who owned the other three pubs on the road all came by to say hello one by one. They were all friendly and well-meaning and everyone got on with one another, you know. It didn't feel like the four of us were rivals for the same drinkers, but more like we were all working together and each had our share of regulars. No one was undercutting the other pubs on prices or anything like that. No, drinks cost what they did and that was that.

People in the flats closest to each pub generally just went to that one. Being as it was a main road running between us, people over the other side went to the other two, and people in the flats our side went to ours or The Duke of Wellington. And if one of us needed something, another pub would help out. If you ran out of beer, you only had to run across or phone round and someone would lend you a barrel. Or they'd come and ask you for something if they ran out.

It was all very neighbourly. You had to be friends really – it wasn't the East End way to do it any differently, other than being helpful and friendly to each other. It provided a good system of security too, as we used to talk to each other about any trouble. So if something kicked off in one of the pubs, the landlord would ring you and say, 'Such and such trouble in so and so pub. Watch they don't come in to you. Be careful.' And then you knew to be on the watch for those people.

But now and again there were a few little mishaps that started in our own pub, like a couple of lads who'd had too much to drink might begin to argue, getting louder and louder. You could always tell when trouble was starting.

That's where my husband was good. He was fearless of people, a real tough guy who was well-known and respected in the area, and he would just go, 'Oi, out! If you want to do anything, do it outside. You've got a big car park out there, so do it out there. Go on, out!' He wouldn't stand for no nonsense. Or if things did get more serious, I've seen Charlie leap the bar. He would be over before you knew it, grabbing 'em by the scruff of the neck and turfing them right out the door like. And that was it. It was over and done with then. I'd try and do it with kindness, saying, 'Come on, love, let's not have a fight,' and that kind of thing. But it was less effective.

Charlie always ended up taking over, and I'd make the call through to the other pubs.

Those kinds of problems mainly happen with youngsters, though, and we didn't get that many young lads in. At other times, it was not as obvious a problem as a fight – you had to have your wits about you. East End wrong 'uns could be as cunning as could be. Not long after we'd opened, it was a lunchtime and I was behind the bar on my own – Charlie had just nipped out on some errand or another. And this woman came in and tapped at the counter. She was about thirty and slim. She seemed very confident and sure of herself.

'Lovey, lovey!' she went.

'Yeah?' I said.

'Charlie about?'

'No.'

'Yeah, I know that really 'cause I just seen him up the road. He turned round and said you've got to give me a fiver 'cause he owes me a fiver.'

'You sure?'

'Oh yeah, 'cause he told me to come in the pub and you'll give it to me.'

'Oh, right. Well, you'll have to hang on for a little while.'

And I stood there for a while trying to think what to do. I couldn't imagine Charlie would have borrowed any money off this woman, but she did seem to know what she was talking about. You didn't have mobiles in them days, and the only phone we had was out in the hallway, but I didn't think I should leave the bar untended to use it – and, to be honest, I wasn't sure where Charlie had gone so I didn't know where to get hold of him anyway.

But as luck would have it, just as I was thinking I would have to give it to her as she had already waited at the bar ten minutes, and it was a bit rude if she had already kindly lent my husband money, Charlie came back.

'That woman there,' I said, 'reckons you owe her a fiver.'

'You what?' He looked at me as though I'd gone daft. 'No way. I don't even know who she is!'

So I turned to her. 'Oh, did you say my husband owed you a fiver?' and 'cause she realized it was him, she completely changed her story.

'Oh no, I remember now, it wasn't here at all.' And off she sauntered out of the pub, not even one bit embarrassed. She was such a chancer, it was flippin' un-believable!

Course, then we worked out that we had just had the sign put up above the door 'Charlie and Pat as licensees' or whatever it was it said, so she had more than likely just read that. Some of the tricks people can come up with, it's unbelievable.

And apparently that woman was no stranger to trying her luck with the other pubs in the area either. I happened to mention about her to one of the women who ran one of the other pubs a few days later, and straight away she knew who I was on about. But unluckily for her, she had actually fallen for it the first time.

Apparently this missus had come in giving her all the hard-up stories as she sat at the bar, and the land-lady had felt sorry for her and given her a couple of drinks. Then the woman had told her, 'And the worst of all in my life right now is my mum died recently, and I can't even bury her. I haven't a penny to bury her with.'

'Well,' the landlady told me, 'I felt so sorry for her I gave her a ten pound note and I said "Now, go bury your mum". Then a few days later I saw her walking along with this elderly woman, who she introduced to me as her mum, all brazen as can be with no hint of shame.' Oh, the cheek!

Yes, she warned me to never take notice of anybody that walked through that door asking me for any money whatsoever, unless I knew them. Because she said people really could come up with some terrible, terrible tricks. They do try to get away with some things. But I don't think we had any others try it on – no one as brazen as her anyhow!

Two people who came in, however, didn't try to hide the fact that they spelt trouble – they wanted me to know they were there, and to make an impression, because they worked on fear. They were two men who worked for the Krays. At that time Ronnie and Reggie Kray were really notorious in the East End. I had known of them for years – it was hard not to – but I hadn't actually met them. Charlie had come across them a couple of times in pubs, but had never had any dealings with them and would just dismiss them when he talked about them as though they were minor thugs. But, of course, that was Charlie's way – the reality, as most people seemed to say, was that they ruled a lot of the East End and were far worse than your average hoodlums.

At the time people had real mixed feelings about them. There were those who said they were good to the old people, always helping them out and treating them and, if you were an East Ender, they had your best interests at heart.

But then there were those who focused on their bad side, who said how violent and intimidating they were, and that they were getting the area a bad reputation.

I mostly didn't give 'em too much thought. I shuddered at some of the stories, but in a strange way could see the glamour and appeal of them – sometimes I'd see pictures of them in the newspapers with some celebrity or another and think they were like celebrities themselves. But my opinion changed a lot when, two years before, Ronnie had shot dead a man called George Cornell as he drank his pint in The Blind Beggar pub in Whitechapel. Ronnie was fearless as anything and didn't care that there were dozens of other drinkers in there. It sounded awful and was the talk of the East End for a long time afterwards. Each day there would be new rumours of what the brothers and their gang had threatened to do to any witness who went forward from the pub that night. And not one person did. But I think that was the time when I, as well as a lot of other people, decided their violent side wasn't right, and I just wanted to keep out of their way.

So on this particular afternoon, I was downstairs serving in the pub on my own, and there were a few of our regular customers in there. I suppose we should have expected a visit from the Krays and their gang at some point as whenever anyone new opened a pub, they would always visit and try their luck. But I have to say, I wasn't prepared.

When these two men came in I knew who they were straight away. Everyone who worked for the Krays had a certain look – all suited and booted, wearing their hats and ties. And they said to me, 'We are working for the Krays. We'd like a word.'

Well, I told 'em it was nothing to do with me and went and got my husband. In true Charlie style, he wasn't afraid and was sure he could handle himself. He just calmly went down to speak to them, and made me go upstairs. We had a buzzer fitted under the counter that went through to upstairs, and he said if he rang it that I was to call the police immediately.

I was scared as anything and sat upstairs shaking like a leaf – after all, these people had a reputation for a reason! But I knew if anyone could deal with them, Charlie could.

Well, I learned afterwards that they had given it all the chat about the strength of the Krays and how it wouldn't be good to get on their bad side, and all that, and then asked him for protection money. I don't know if they asked directly or just hinted at it, but Charlie told 'em to piss off! And let's say he showed them a few bits and pieces he had behind the counter, which I think, combined with his size and fierceness, made them realize it wouldn't be worth their while. When I say bits and pieces, I mainly mean this great big truncheon he had that he kept in case of any serious trouble. He had trousers specially made with a side pocket down the leg to keep it in, and he'd always tap it and say, 'If anyone starts, I'll give them one of these.'

So Charlie didn't have to press the buzzer, and the two men left. And although I worried about it for a while after, they never did come back and try to cause any trouble.

Other pubs in the area were paying them, though. Not everyone, but a lot of them, 'cause they preferred to do that than risk trouble. But if you knew one of them or were cute enough, you could get away with it. And I guess Charlie was.

THREE

Life Upstairs

As for life upstairs in the pub, well, it was like a different world. It was a world ruled by the kids, and it was hectic. The kids weren't allowed down into the pub, so I spent half my time running up from the bar to see what they were up to, and each time I did, who knew what I would find. But then again five lively kids full of energy, left to their own devices . . . it can only be expected.

Though it was a big place, we only had three bedrooms upstairs – one for me and Charlie, one for the three girls to share, and one for the two boys. Then there was a big dining room, all posh like, that we called the best room! It had a big dining table and chairs, and that's where Charlie would hold meetings, say, if the managers from the brewery or other local publicans wanted to come round to discuss anything. There was even a portable bar in there that he had bought and that was kept well stocked for when he was entertaining.

The brewery linked to the pub was Watney Mann, although people still called it Mann, Crossman and Paulin, which was one of the two original breweries that merged to make Watney Mann. M, C & P was based in the East End, in Whitechapel, and you can still see the old brewery building if you pass over that way. Although it has since been turned into a Sainsbury's, I think the original M, C & P sign is still there. It was a well enough respected brewery anyhow, one that we were proud to put on our business cards to encourage people to come to The Rising Sun.

The meetings that took place in the best room were weekly, I think, but Charlie really guarded that room. There was no way any of the kids were ever allowed to set foot in there. It was off limits.

Then there was the kitchen, which was pretty ordinary with all the basics, and what I guess was the sitting room, though it was used for just about anything but sitting. It was a great big room over the back of the pub, where the kids used to play and watch the telly, and mostly entertain themselves.

But I tell you what, I had more three-piece suites in my time in the pub than you can imagine. I'm not kidding you, they were always being broken, split or torn during games the children played, especially Little Charlie who was forever jumping from one to the other. I was out shopping for a new one every couple of months. There was a big dining table and chairs in there too, which is where we used to eat our meals.

And then at the end of the hallway was another staircase that led up to a loft. That was like the kids' play area, and they had toys and what have you up there. With all that space the kids were quite spoiled really!

They even had a mini boxing ring up there that Charlie had helped them build. He was an ex-boxer himself and obsessed with the sport. He was forever following matches and could watch it for hours on the television. Charlie was keen for the boys to go down the same route, and built the ring so they could mess around in it play fighting. Although I remember one time my dad and Charlie encouraged them to fight for real when they were only about five and six, and Stephen clumped Charlie and clean on knocked him out! It sounds really bad and it would probably be seen as the wrong thing to do now, encouraging your kids to fight each other, but back then boxing was a big part of East End life for lads of all ages.

Anyhow, to give 'em their dues, the kids were well behaved in a lot of ways. They all had their bedtimes, and mostly stuck to them. Maybe because they were afraid of the consequences if they didn't!

If I thought they weren't settling for me when they should be, I'd come down and say to Charlie, all worn out like, 'Charl', you better go up and make sure they're going to bed.' But he didn't even have to get that far. He'd just stand at the bottom of the stairs and in a loud, strict-sounding voice, he'd go, 'You in bed?' and you'd just hear all this scurrying and then silence. And there wouldn't be a peep out of 'em for the rest of the evening. It was obvious he was the stronger, scarier parent, there for the discipline, whereas I was the soft touch in the kids' eyes.

Sometimes I was glad he could discipline them. Days when they were too much of a handful, or one of them had done something naughty but they wouldn't own up which one, I'd say, 'Wait till your father comes in.' And when he got back all five of them would get a clout. He didn't bother trying to find out who it was – he worked on the idea that the others would punish whoever had done it for getting them all a whack! So one by one, they'd all get a smack on the leg. But it was only ever a smack or a slap by hand – he never used anything to hit them with.

It would put an end to whatever they were doing anyhow. Other times too, say, if we were all in the car and one of the boys started whingeing and ruining the journey for everyone else, Charlie would stop the car, give them a good clump and that was it. They would stop their moaning quickly enough and we could get on with the journey in peace. I think the kids respected him for it really.

I know the threat of a smack from Charlie, who had these great big hands, much bigger than ordinary, was a good deterrent for the kids – they reckon his slaps used to have a real sting. But when they were misbehaving, I don't think it did 'em any harm. Matter of fact, I would give the boys a good smack or a wallop from time to time if they needed it too, though I don't think I ever hit the girls.

And I did try and protect them from Charlie sometimes, when I didn't think what they had done was too bad but I knew Charlie would disagree. So I'd be like, 'Don't let your father know', 'cause I knew they'd be in for it and I'd feel sorry for them if they had a clout coming. But he had a sixth sense for when something was going on, and he'd jump down my throat if I hadn't told him. 'What they done?' he'd yell. It was a real juggling act sometimes, getting Charlie to control the kids but stopping him being too hard on them.

After we moved into the pub the children quickly became independent, as no matter how involved we tried to be with their lives, it was inevitable that they ended up looking after themselves a lot more than they had when we lived in Bray Drive. So with things like bathing, even though I'd make sure they were clean, they'd just get on and do it themselves of an evening.

And when they had homework to do, they got on with it, without me having to chase them. They didn't get a lot of homework, mind, not like the amount kids seem to be loaded down with today, but they still got some. And they'd come home from school and do it straight away so they could get on and play afterwards, or sometimes they would stay at school after hours and do it there to get it out the way before coming home. Or at least Susan and Carol did that – June, meantime, was proving more difficult. She couldn't stand school. She took a dislike to it from her first day and would do anything she could to avoid it.

Some mornings she would tell me she didn't feel well, and although I didn't always believe her, I'd let her have a couple of days off. Other times I'd send her off to school of a morning and she'd reappear an hour later. And a couple of times I found out she had gone round a mate's house and spent the day there. There was a thing called the School Board that would come round and ask about her and find out where she had been. But they didn't really do anything – just checked I knew she had been off, wrote it in their book, and left again.

Well, we tried so many times, and her dad used to get furious at the rebellious streak in her, but in the end we near on gave up. And all along, if I'm honest, I suppose I knew where she was coming from, having hardly been a fan, or regular attendee, of school myself when I was younger.

I suppose they were real latchkey kids, and most of the time just got on with things themselves. They didn't get themselves into any real wrong doings thankfully – more like scrapes than anything else. Not that we always noticed!

There is one time Stephen likes to bring up when he's trying to play the sympathy card and make me feel like I neglected him. He went out with a few of his friends to play – I'm not sure I even knew he had gone, or if he just took himself off and sneaked out – but they went into a lift in a housing block the other side of the main road, and then the lift got stuck. Apparently they were in there for a couple of hours before the fire brigade arrived and rescued them. Poor Stephen says he was so frightened that as soon as the doors opened he just put his head down and ran, as it was just his instinct to get home. Well, he had to dodge across that busy road – which wasn't as bad as today now it's become the

Blackwall Tunnel Northern Approach – but it was still scary enough for a young lad to cross by himself, and he dashed back into the pub and up the stairs. And you know what? Not one of us had even missed him or noticed he was gone.

I felt guilty at times that I couldn't be there for the children as much as I would have liked, but that's how it was. We had to make a living, and anyhow life at the time meant that most other parents were in a similar situation to us. And I don't think it did the kids any harm really.

All the children had turned into quite individual characters by this time. June was good at helping me out with the younger ones, getting them fed and off to bed. But she had quite a temper on her, and when she got angry she couldn't half torment the other children.

Susan was quieter and more studious, and she cried the most easily out of them. She was terrified of feathers and birds, which gave June a field day when she wanted to wind her up. Susan was the best behaved of the girls and quite hard working.

Then there was Carol. Well, it was becoming clear she was a bit of a cheeky one. But she was quite the little princess as well, so somehow she got away with it. When she was younger anyhow! Susan and Carol were closer out of the girls, I'd say, perhaps because they were closer in age.

As for the boys, they were typical brothers, who got on well but were always bickering and fighting too. Stephen was the more sensible and thoughtful of the two, whereas Charlie, well, he was a cheeky little scamp. But he had such a way about him that you never knew whether to hug him or hit him!

I tell you, those kids didn't half keep me on my toes. As an East End landlady, a sugar girl and a mum of five very different but equally wonderful kids, there was never a dull moment in my life!

FOUR

Cutting Back

After we had been there for two or three months, I was right exhausted and didn't think I could take any more of it. It wasn't that I didn't like the pub – it had actually grown on me a lot more than I thought it would. But working there, looking after the kids and doing the factory shifts was just too much. So we sat down and did the maths and decided I would give up the factory, and that we'd also take on a barmaid and a cleaner.

I can't say I was sorry to see the back of Tate & Lyle. It was a nice enough place to work and I'd made a few friends there by that time, but the hours were too much. I just couldn't do it no more. And unlike in the past when I had left a few times but somehow always ended up back there, this time I really did leave for good.

As for the barmaid, I forget how Charlie found her now, whether she was recommended or we advertised or what, but we took on this girl called Juliette. She was French and in her twenties, and I thought she was very good. She was single, so happy to work as many hours as I needed, and she was sociable and chatty with the regulars – she did have a French accent, but had been over here for a good few years, so it wasn't too strong that people struggled to understand her!

And we got this cleaner then too. She was an elderly lady called Winnie, who was very hard working. She would come in and clean all downstairs in the pub – that's all we had hired her to do – but then she'd say to me, 'Do you need any help upstairs?' 'cause she knew I had my hands full.

I'd shake my head and say, 'No, no, It's all fine.'

But she'd just give me this knowing look and say, 'Yes, you do. Come on, I'll come up, I don't want paying.'

Though I always tried to protest, I was secretly pleased, and she'd come up and help me with a bit of washing or to make the beds. Although over time I got the kids to make their own – you didn't have duvets and covers back then. It was just blankets and sheets so it was easy enough for the little 'uns to just pull them over themselves. And then of course I'd end up paying Winnie 'cause I'd feel too guilty not to. So we both benefited from it really.

It was also around this time that we changed the

layout of the pub a bit. Hardly anyone went in the snug, so we decided it was a waste of space. I suppose there were fewer people who felt the need to hide when they were in the pub, but also the habit of getting a pint to take away was becoming more rare. We came to the conclusion we'd be better with one single, bigger bar, so we had it all knocked into one. We got the brewery people to come in and do it, and they got rid of the wall in between and gave the place a fresh lick of paint so it looked much better after. I always felt that it gave it even more of a kind of family friendly feel – not that kids were allowed in at that time still. No kids under fourteen were allowed in pubs until the law changed to permit it in 1995 – long after we were out of the pub trade.

Women, though, did start coming into The Rising Sun around this time. Still nothing like today where you are as likely to see a group of girls in a pub as a group of lads. But it was no longer frowned upon for a woman to go to a pub with a man – the culture was changing. So you started to see women come in, mostly with their husbands or boyfriends at a weekend, and sit at a table having a quiet drink.

But, as I said before, wine wasn't a thing really sold in pubs then, so women went for other drinks. There was a Snowball – an advocaat and lemonade cocktail – and Babycham, which is a sparkling pear drink that came in a small bottle. Older women would have a Guinness or a milk stout – a stout mixed with lactose that comes from milk, which you can still get in some country pubs today. The women would always swear by it and say that it did them the world of good. But the drink women would go for the most was gin. Gin and orange, gin and bitter lemon, or gin and tonic.

Oh, but my, sometimes it was not a pretty sight. These women were not used to drinking, and whereas today a girl will knock back a bottle of wine without thinking twice, back then three or four glasses of gin and orange and, oh, it would all go wrong. They'd suddenly be sat there and start crying their eyes out. The tears would come down as they went back through the years and what had happened, telling all their stories of their troubles. Their poor husband or boyfriend would be sat there trying to comfort them, or in some cases getting annoyed, but mainly just looking around completely embarrassed.

We'd see it starting and give the man a sympathetic glance, then me and Charlie would look at each other and say, 'Oh, there she goes, the tears are out. She's had more than enough. Look at 'er!' They used to say 'gin's a woman's ruin' and, watching all those women, I'd say I have to agree.

I never used to drink at that time, except for the odd

shandy behind the bar if I was 'specially gasping and didn't feel like a lemonade. I had the kids to see to and, to be honest, seeing the state of those women kind of put me off!

But I remember one time, a few years later, when I had a drink with a friend and for some reason I thought I'd give gin a go. Next thing I knew, ugh . . . never no more! True enough, it does all come back, and I was just the same with all that crying business, going over the sad times in my childhood when my mum died and when I fell out with my dad over meeting Charlie.

Oh, it was awful. Then the next morning I had a headache, a hangover I suppose, and I said to myself, 'What was that all about, you daft woman? What were you crying for?'

But I can tell you one thing – I've never been drunk on gin since!

Charlie had been out the night before and not seen me, but the next morning he said, 'What's wrong with you?' When I told him, he laughed and said, 'It's your own fault, you stupid woman!'

'Cause he never got hangovers, never once, no matter how much he drank. Or if he felt bad, he never let on, but would sort it out with another pint the next morning – hair of the dog as we called it.

And he'd drink behind the bar pretty much every

night. Not that he would have drunk gin, though. No, the only spirits a man would drink were whisky and rum. Charlie was a fan of whisky, although he always liked a pint of bitter as well. He loved a drink did my husband. But it never affected his work. No, he was as sharp as ever with the money and reckoning up what we had sold. He'd be behind the bar, knocking back pints, chatting with the locals, even singing, but he still knew what was what. He wasn't silly. I'd be writing things down like mad – phew! But he kept it all in his head. Didn't matter how drunk he was – he could fall over and still know how many bottles of Guinness or whatever he'd sold.

Sundays were always my favourite day in the pub. I think it was because it was the day people were most relaxed and friendly. And our hours on a Sunday were a wee bit different, with us opening the doors from 12.30 until 3 p.m., and then again from 5 until 10 p.m., even though our working day started long before that.

Charlie and Dad would head off to the Old Billingsgate fish market on Lower Thames Street every Sunday morning for about 6 a.m. It was in a huge, beautiful old building down on the river, with a high ceiling that was filled with men shouting, and a real hustle and bustle to it. It was known as the best place to go to get fresh fish in London, and although it's been turned into a fancy conference and exhibition centre in recent years, at least the building looks the same as it ever did.

Anyway, they'd get a box of the best prawns available – course, Dad being from a fish family, he knew how to tell the best ones, as well as how to get the best deals. In fact, I think the trip down there was more of a social visit for them to catch up with old friends. Then they'd bring the prawns back and I'd have to shell them and wash them properly in vinegar, before putting them out on the counter for everyone to have a nibble on with cocktail sticks when the bar opened at midday.

Sunday was also the day I sometimes had June down working in the pub with me, and she occasionally did Saturdays too – she helped out at the weekend as and when we needed it. She began giving us a hand during the week as well from time to time, say, for an hour or so on the odd evening. Now, I know you are going to say how could she when she was only twelve or so at the time and shouldn't have been allowed to work in the pub. And I know that, but we couldn't afford to get no more help than Juliette, and at times at the weekend it was so busy we needed help and it was the only way we could get it.

Mainly, she did the washing up. Them days you didn't

have a machine to wash the glasses – instead you would put them in water and brush them, then set them out to drain. Then, when we were busier, she would serve too and get the beers out of the fridge for customers. But I had to swear blind she was eighteen. Terrible, I know! I even used to do what I could to make her look older – I'd put her in older-looking clothes, and I had this awful green eye shadow that I used to paint on her before she came down. We even had a wig that someone had given us that we put on her, so she ended up looking like a right ol' girl! The locals mostly knew how old she was, though, but they didn't care. So long as she could help get them a drink, that was all that mattered!

She had a sharp mind and could do the maths on the till, so we let her serve the locals and take their money. And she loved it. She was good at it, and I think she felt quite at home as a barmaid.

Anyway, so we'd be there serving the drinks while the customers munched on their prawns, and I'd sometimes put out cheese and biscuits too. Then an hour or two later I'd put out bowls of roast potatoes, again for people to help themselves to for free like. It was just a nice thing for the regulars to have with their pints.

The other corner pubs used to do similar things. All of us would put out food of some sort. One even put out fresh bread, a great big long baguette cut into thin slices. And they'd put out pieces of cut-up meat too so that customers could make themselves a kind of sandwich.

To be honest, I reckon that if you'd have done a pub crawl around all four pubs, you could have as good as got your dinner that way! And some of the more cheeky drinkers did just that. They'd come in, order just the one drink – a lemonade or a shandy – and eat a whole bowl of potatoes and get their belly full, then walk out and head on to the next pub. You'd never see them no more that day. It was a bit of a flippin' liberty really!

Meantime, I'd also be trying to cook food for a family Sunday lunch. 'Cause Sunday was the one day I tried to make sure we all ate as a family, in the gap when the pub shut between three and five o'clock. We'd all sit down together and have a roast, and I tried to make that happen every week without fail.

Family mealtimes during the week just weren't happening as often as I'd have liked, though. I cooked all the meals for everyone, and when I could I'd take time and cook the family favourite – jellied eels or stewed eels, which Charlie especially loved – but it was usually a case of each of us grabbing something to eat when we could. A lot of the time I'd have to leave it to June to make sure the kids had all eaten.

I didn't half feel guilty about that. Then, even worse, sometimes when it got too busy I would find it would be time for their dinner and realize I'd not made anything. So I'd just have to run upstairs and give them money to go down to the caf' down the road to have something to eat. Luckily that didn't happen often, but I hated it when I did – I was looking after my locals in the pub, but feeling I was neglecting my kids upstairs.

And clearly I wasn't the only person who wasn't getting to do the family dinner as often as they'd like either. Oh, I'll never forget the day one of our regulars got told off for the same thing . . .

George was a nice enough fella. He was about forty and was a stocky chap with a bit of a belly. He always used to sit up at the bar and drink his pint, sometimes chatting with us, sometimes preferring to sit quietly. One Sunday he was there as usual, with his pint sat in front of him, and I suppose he had been there a couple of hours. Well, as it turned out, that was a couple of hours more than his wife could cope with, 'cause suddenly this big lady came storming through the door of the pub. She was carrying a bundle under her arm covered in a tea towel, and she marched straight up to George.

Everyone stopped to look 'cause it didn't take a genius to see just how furious she was.

'Sitting in 'ere all bleedin' day long? Well, you can eat your f***ing dinner in here an' all! Here, now get on with it!'

And with that she slammed her bundle down in front of him, which turned out to be a plate with a roast dinner on it.

Well, we were all just staring, and the whole place had gone dead quiet as we waited to see what our regular would do about it.

Then brazen as could be, he just turned to her and went, 'Oh, thanks, girl, lovely! Thanks very much! Now, did you get me a knife and fork as well?'

Oh dear, well that was it. I near on died trying to stop myself laughing. We were all fighting to control ourselves, but you wouldn't dare let her see you laughing because she was a big woman like. So I ducked down behind the bar, pretending to get something, so I could have a silent laugh without her seeing.

Oh, I couldn't believe his cheek, and she gave him such a look before going out and slamming the door behind her. We all just exploded. I'll never forget that, it was so funny. I mean, I had sympathy for the poor woman, but the way George answered her . . . It became a laugh and a joke after that, though, you know. Our regular greeting to him became, 'You all right for your dinner tonight?'

Oh, it can't have been an easy marriage that one, for either of them. Nor was my own always proving easy in the pub.

Charlie's jealous streak, which had always been there, properly came into its own in The Rising Sun. Oh, he was a very jealous man. The amount of nights he accused me of all sorts. Me! I was probably the most unflirty landlady in the whole of the East End! It wasn't my thing. I had my husband and my family – they were what mattered – and I had no interest in any man turning my head. But Charlie couldn't see that and was always on the look out for something that would prove otherwise to him, 'specially after a few drinks.

'You made eyes at that man, didn't you? I saw you make eye contact with him at the end o' the bar,' he'd say.

'What? I'm serving in the pub, Charlie!' I'd screech back, frustrated.

'Yeah, I know, I know. Look at him, he's after you.'

'Oh, for God's sake, Charl, do you really think—'

'I know. I've seen it. He winked at ya. You winked back at him, didn't you?'

'I don't even—'

At times my life was a misery. I guess on the one hand it was nice, as despite being married for all those years, he obviously still cared and thought I was attractive enough that another man would be after me. But on the other hand . . . oh, it was so wearing!

If a punter would say, 'Have a drink for yourself like. Go on, don't matter about the change,' which was a common way to tip in them days, you could see Charlie's ears prick up and he'd be by my side in an instant.

'You better not. Don't take a drink off of him 'cause you might give the wrong idea,' and he'd be poking me, like in the side at the same time.

But I'd ignore Charlie and go, 'OK, thanks very much,' and I used to just take the money – well, I was hardly going to turn it down. But I'd get bad looks off Charlie for the next while, and I'd think to myself, 'Oh, he's a sod!'

It was embarrassing, though, and I'm sure the customers could see what was going on. His rib-poking was hardly subtle! In fact, knowing some of the cheekier ones, they probably only offered me a drink to wind him up!

The upside was that he never stayed mad about it for long. He'd have his fit for a few minutes, then sulk for another ten minutes or so, but then it would be forgotten. It had to be or it would have been impossible for us to have kept things running behind the bar. The need to work took over from his daft ideas, thank goodness!

All this makes it sound like me and Charlie were always at each other, but despite our ups and downs we were generally happy. He could drive me crazy, but I wouldn't have changed him for the world!

FIVE

Now, That's Entertainment!

The longer we were in the pub, the more creative and adventurous the kids became with the games they dreamt up and the ways they entertained themselves. Looking back, they did well in some ways. I mean, they were left to make their own entertainment, so I could hardly blame them when they did . . .

I remember there was one game they invented where they would pour water all over the wooden floors in their play room and pretend they were ice skating over it. Can you imagine?! Other times they would dress Charlie up as a little girl and stick him in a pram, pretending he was a baby, and push him around. I don't know whether he went along with it because he was good natured or because, as the youngest, he had no choice!

On our first Bonfire Night in the pub, they dressed

him as a guy with a mask and all that and put him in the pram outside the pub, asking 'a penny for the guy' from passers-by. Well, they were as pleased as could be when they came back in to tell us that some people had given them money, 'specially one bloke who drove past and threw a coin out the window for them. They had a scramble to find it, and when they did, it was an old thrupenny bit, which was quite a lot of money in them days.

In the sitting room upstairs we had chairs that were on casters, and the five children would take it in turn to push each other around sat in them, imagining they were on the waltzer at the fun fair. The bangs and squeaks I would hear through the ceiling when I was downstairs . . . oh, it made my mind go crazy!

Some nights, though, things would go silent, and you knew they had finally found something worth watching on TV. But sometimes they'd choose something that was a bit too much for them. A couple of times I went upstairs and would find the five of them trying to sleep in one bed together as they were too frightened to sleep on their own after watching a horror film!

One game they had, though, the one they loved the most, was playing Bus, but oh, it nearly got them in some serious trouble. We had this great big cabinet up there, a kind of wall unit, made up of all this square shelving that was built to look a bit like boxes. It was ever such a big thing and covered the best part of one wall, and it was filled with ornaments and glass.

Well, they treated it as though it was their bus. Charlie was always the driver, and used to sit in this little cupboard bit of it down the bottom – I can still see it now. One of them would be the ticket inspector, and they even had an actual machine that issued tickets that we had got off someone, so it really helped their imaginations go mad. The rest of them would pretend to be the passengers, and would climb into other sections of the cabinet to buy their tickets and find a seat. Oh, they had hours of fun, and pretended to go to all sorts of places.

But this one night, we were working in the pub downstairs as usual when we heard such a bang from upstairs that I thought the ceiling was about to cave in. We all looked at each other in the bar, and I went running up the stairs, faster than I ever had, with Charlie close behind, as well as some of the locals.

Well, when we got in there we saw what had happened – the whole unit had started rocking, and then completely gone, fallen right off the wall and crashed on to the floor. And at first I couldn't see any of the kids and was panicking and like 'Oh my God!' But then they crawled out from under the wreckage, and we saw they were all fine, except Charlie. We couldn't see him anywhere. I could feel the panic building in my chest, and grabbed on to Big Charlie's arm, needing him to do something.

Carol started screaming, 'Charlie's going to die!' and it was complete mayhem, I tell you.

He was trapped under the unit with the doors closed around him, so we had to try and move it and, bless him, we found him curled up in a ball. But was he hurt and scared? Nope, not a bit was our Little Charlie!

As brazen as anything, he went, 'I was a good driver, weren't I, Mum?'

Oh, I could have smacked him.

'I'll give you a bleeding good driver! I'll kill you if you ever do that again!' I yelled. He was a little sod was he.

Meantime, Big Charlie was hardly being an angel. My husband was the most sensible, intelligent, down-to-earth person – most of the time. But occasionally he could be as stubborn and unthinking as can be. One of his habits that frustrated me to my absolute wits' end was his way of doing things on the spur of the moment. Not that I mind the odd surprise, but Charlie would get a thought in his head sometimes and not think a thing of the consequences, only whether it was a good thing then and there.

The perfect example of this was one Easter – I think it was the year we moved in to the pub – when I was panicking. I had been so busy I'd hardly noticed Easter creeping up on me, and I said to Charlie, 'Oh, I've got no Easter eggs for the kids. I need to go and get them, though I can't see when I'll have time.'

'I'll go,' he replied. 'I'll get them. You've no need to worry.'

Now, I'm sure that at that moment he did actually have every intention of getting eggs. But somewhere along the road between the pub and the shop, he got a new idea into his head. Typical Charlie – a lot of the time he'd go to the shop and come back with something very different from what I'd asked him to get. And this time he decided to take himself off to Petticoat Lane, a market in the East End, and bring back a present of a different sort.

Petticoat Lane was a really lively, noisy, busy market, where you could find just about anything you were after – plus a lot more! The stallholders were always full of the chat, and would gather plenty of crowds as they showed off their wares. There was all sorts of wheeling and dealing went on there. Which is probably why Charlie made a beeline down there. So an hour later he came back through the door with his coat pulled over, hiding something.

'What you got there?' I asked. All of a sudden I became suspicious like. 'That don't look like eggs!'

'Oh, forget the eggs,' he said. I've got something better than that. Look.'

And he opened his coat to show me a little Alsatian puppy.

Well, I went mad. 'Who wants a bleedin' dog! The kids want Easter eggs! As if I haven't got enough on my hands, you think I'm gonna look after a dog now too?'

And I didn't half swear at him. But in true Charlie fashion, his mind was made up and there was no changing it. He just shrugged and told me, 'Well, they'll like this better.' And that was the end of the conversation.

I had a secret theory, though, that it was Charlie's revenge on me for not letting him have any more kids! Maybe he thought a dog would cause just as much chaos for me. I think he knew we had our hands full with the five children, but every now and then he would try his luck. But you know what I used to say? 'If you want any more, you can go with 'er next door.'

That used to tickle me, and was an old saying of mine that I always used. I say it to my daughters and granddaughters now when they have had enough kids. 'If he wants any more, send him to 'er next door.' It always gets a laugh!

But sure enough, Charlie was right about the dog being a popular present, and all the kids fell in love with him straight away. He was so young – he was just a little bundle of fur then really – and, I admit, I got a bit of a soft spot for him as well in the end.

He got named Rex, I've no idea who by or why, but before long he was well and truly one of the family. He wasn't an aggressive dog at all. Although I remember one day soon after we got him when it was hot, so Rex was probably all bothered, and the kids were messing around next to him. Then Little Charlie fell on him, and Rex snapped and bit his ear. He didn't draw blood – it was more a reaction than anything – but my husband wanted to make sure Rex knew who was boss and that he couldn't do that again. So can you believe what he did? He got Charlie to bite the dog back on the ear! Well, it sounds odd, I know, but it worked. It was the first and last time he ever snapped at any of the kids.

We kept him upstairs and he just roamed around up there – he was a family pet rather than one for the pub. Besides, people are quite often scared of Alsatians when they don't know them, so we didn't want to frighten the customers away! Not that there was anything to be afraid of with Rex. He was an amazing and friendly dog with a really good nature.

We had a few other pets while we were in the pub

too. I don't remember where any of 'em came from, but no doubt they were whims of Charlie's too! And definitely something aimed at keeping the children entertained upstairs, as well as teaching them how to look after things. We had a goldfish bowl with a few fish in it that the kids were supposed to feed, though I am sure I ended up doing it more often than not. Then there was Joey the budgerigar, who sat in a cage in the corner of the sitting room but was never allowed out of his cage to fly around as, like I said, Susan was afraid of birds, so she'd have been petrified if he'd been fluttering around the room. That was the threat June always made to Susan, though, when she got annoyed with her: 'Behave, or I'll let the budgie out.'

Poor Susan would end up in floods of tears!

There seemed to be no end to the ways the kids found to entertain themselves while Charlie and I were behind the bar serving the punters.

There was an outside area to The Rising Sun with a veranda, but it wasn't used that much 'cause the weather was rarely that good, and as people could smoke inside there wasn't the need for it the way there is today. Then there were steps from that down to the massive great car park that belonged to the pub.

I found out later that the kids used to sit upstairs

banging on the windows, and when they got the attention of people on the veranda, they'd stick their tongues out at them and pull faces. They were a naughty lot!

But a couple of years later when Susan started secondary school she was left red-faced about it. One day a girl came up and said to her, 'I know you. Your mum and dad used to own The Rising Sun and you used to bang on the window and stick your tongue out!'

Oh, she was embarrassed then. A small world – but it serves her right!

And then we had what we called our own garden, but it was really like a back yard. All the empty beer bottles and crates would go there, and at the back were railings and a little bit of a grass verge blocking us off from the river. It was The River Lea, though over the years the bit around our way had been made to look like a canal, with locks, and concrete edging – I suppose as it was used so much by industry and that.

You used to get the barges come through, transporting all sorts of things for the factories roundabouts. The one place I particularly remember was the flour mills just across the river, the Sun Flour Mills they were called, in St Leonard's Street. And they used to transport their flour up and down the river, their boats going back and forth at all hours of the day and night.

One story everyone used to tell about those mills

was how they had blown up just two or three years before we took over the pub. From what I understand, flour dust in the air suddenly exploded, but I have no idea how, or what the science is behind it. I just know it happened, and it was enough to destroy part of the mills, as well as bits of buildings around them, and across the river even. A lorry was crushed when one of the walls collapsed, and sadly four people were killed and thirty-one were injured. It was a big thing in the local area and was in all the papers at the time. It was still something people were talking about, even by the time we took over The Rising Sun a few years after it had happened.

Well, at six o' clock in a morning the workers from the river would call up at the pub. They would be the port pilots, who guided the boats in and out on the river, or security guards and workers from the flour factory. We also had what were known as lightermen, the chaps who would steer small boats up and down the rivers and canals in the area, carrying goods from big ships to the factories and quaysides and back again. They didn't have motors on their boats – they only had a steering paddle and had to use the currents and the tides.

Charlie would get up and let them in – there would only be half a dozen of them at most, and they'd sit and have a couple of drinks and a chat with him for an hour or so. The people who owned the pub before us had done it for them, so it was just like a tradition that we kept going. They were men who had been at work from the day before and through the night, and their shift was just finishing at 6 a.m. We just used to think why shouldn't they be allowed a drink before heading home, even if it was a different hour to everyone else? They still needed a chance to unwind and relax before they had to go to sleep.

Well, there was one other person who was keen to get involved with these men of a morning and that was Little Charlie.

Yep, the minute he heard them arrive he'd be up and out of bed, and he'd head straight downstairs, still in his pyjamas. We didn't let the kids in the bar that often, but it was different at that time of the day.

And dear Charlie would go into the bar, bold as brass, put his feet up on a chair and say, 'Hello there. Hello mate. I'll have a pint.'

Oh, the lightermen loved him and would torment him and encourage him as bad as anything.

'Go on, Charlie, have another drop. Have another one.' They'd tease him, even though the poor lad was only five or six years old!

And Big Charlie played along and would give him a drink of lemonade. And Little Charlie didn't notice – bless him, he really believed he was getting a beer. While the two Charlies were seeing to the river workers, I'd be upstairs getting the other kids ready for school, but I'd pass through sometimes and see Little Charlie, sat there as though he was one of the gang, happy as can be with a pint in his hand. I'd often hear him say, 'Pass me another pint,' as I walked past!

One time he did end up with a real pint in his hand, though. We had shut the pub up for the afternoon, then realized we couldn't find Charlie anywhere. We searched high and low and were starting to get worried, though we knew he had to be in there somewhere.

Finally, we went back down to the pub and, no word of a lie, he was there by a fruit machine with a load of coins and a pint of lager! Putting coins in, pulling the lever down, sipping on a pint of lager. It was terrible, but I had to laugh. And his behaviour ain't stopped to this day!

The other kids would come down into the pub at other times, when it was quieter of an evening, but as soon as it got busy, we sent them back upstairs.

But one day Charlie took his belief that he was one of those workers a step too far, venturing right down to the river itself. He knew he wasn't supposed to be there – all the kids knew the river was off limits. It was deep and the last thing we wanted was them trying to swim in it, or falling in. So we always said to them to keep away. No, they weren't allowed to go anywhere near it.

But of course if anyone was going to ignore that, it was Little Charlie. He headed off down there, but luckily for everyone his dad spotted him. He was there at the railings, which were the only thing stopping him get from our yard to the river, and he was trying to clamber through. He had got as far as one leg, when my husband caught him.

I'll tell you, his dad gave him a good hiding for that one. He was determined Charlie would take notice 'cause he could quite easily have got killed.

Well, after he'd been smacked, Little Charlie went upstairs and we went back to whatever we were doing in the pub. I think it was open at the time, so we had customers to serve. Anyhow, all of a sudden the police arrived. Bow Road Police Station was nearby and a copper stomped in, followed by a policewoman.

'Mr and Mrs Brooker?' he asked, all formal like.

'Yes.'

'Charles Brooker? I understand you have smacked your boy.'

In them days you were allowed to smack your kid and, fair enough, with the likes of Little Charlie, a lot of the time it was necessary. So we didn't know why that mattered. But more so, how did they know?!

'What the—? Who told you that?!' We were rightly confused.

'You've been cruel to him as well, it has been reported. Could we come in and see him?'

My husband told me to stay downstairs with the customers and he took the police up, and I was just left there thinking, 'Whatever's going on?'

Well, it turns out, without us knowing, Charlie had called the police himself after he went upstairs. Oh, the embarrassment. Not that Little Charlie felt it. He wasn't the slightest bit shy or ashamed of what he had done.

'My dad hit me one,' he said, as soon as he saw the copper.

'Why did he hit you?'

'Because I went and tried to get through the railings by the river.'

'So that's why your dad done that then?'

'Yeah. Put him away in prison, will you?' he said to the policeman, looking at him, expecting it to happen. Can you believe him? The boy was the cheekiest little sod.

But instead the clever copper leant forward and whack! – he gave Little Charlie another smack on his bum. 'Now you've got one from me too for doing that. Don't never do it again, you hear?'

Oh, Little Charlie couldn't get over that. He never

forgave that policeman! Not that it stopped him trying to boast to us. As soon as I went upstairs he told me, 'See, Mum, I did phone the police, didn't I? I nearly got you arrested.'

It was just the latest in the naughty Charlie stories ... but at least the other kids could rely on him for some fun and entertainment!

SIX

A Thief Among Us

Life in the pub was relentless. You never got a day off, 'cause how were you supposed to? It's not like you could just shut the place up for a few days. The locals wouldn't be happy about that. And there was no one we could leave to run it for us. We even opened each year on Christmas Day, which I was right unhappy about. Most of the pubs didn't open up, but of course Charlie had to, and all the locals were so pleased that every Tom, Dick and Harry would be in. Then we'd spend the day standing behind the bar, and we didn't even get our own Christmas dinner 'cause I didn't get a second to cook it. That was the bit I hated most – not being able to sit down on Christmas Day with Charlie and the kids to have that family meal. The kids would just end up entertaining themselves upstairs, as though it was any other day of the year, while we worked downstairs.

In fact, the most time I ever got away from the place was my weekly trip to the hairdresser's. Back then people would get their hair done once a week. Not cut or coloured or anything, just washed and styled. And preferably styled in a way that was fashionable, but also practical, so it stayed out of the way and you didn't need to do anything with it until the next week when you were back at the hairdresser's.

Well, my ginger hair was really long at this time, and I took to having it in this big bun on top of my head – a beehive as it was called. Each week I would go to a local salon and they'd wash my hair and put it all up on the top of my head, pinning it like mad until it wasn't going to move anywhere. Then I had to keep it like that. So I'd be lying in bed in all sorts of funny positions and getting a stiff neck – anything to protect my hair! I wouldn't dare get it messed up. Through the week I would kind of brush it up to make it look fresher, but I would never try and actually do the style myself. Although, occasionally, it would go wrong before the week was out, and I'd need to go round there and say to my hairdresser, 'Quick, do it in,' and she'd push it in with a few more clips so it wouldn't move for rest of the week.

But that was the only effort we really had time to make with our appearance. Now people dress themselves up, trying to look younger or more glamorous. But we didn't have time, and a lot of what is on offer today wasn't even an option then. Can you imagine me trying to fit in a trip to the nail or tanning salon in between everything else I had to do? No, I think not!

As for the kids' hair, I wanted to keep them all with short, cropped hair – the girls too – for two main reasons. Firstly, it was much easier. Life was too hectic for me to be finding the time to brush their hair daily and plait it or whatever. And the other reason was health – there was less chance of them getting nits that way. Anything like that with the five kids would have been a nightmare.

Opposite the pub was a liver sausage factory. For some reason that I can't remember now, inside the factory was also what was like a training college that taught all sorts of things. One bit was a hair salon for trainee hair-dressers so it was much cheaper than an ordinary one. So sometimes I'd send the kids across there to have their hair cut and other times I'd send them to my hairdresser's, but they always had their hair cut about once a month to keep it short.

Looking back, it was funny, though. They all had their hair the same and were all dressed in the same clothes. It was normal then, and most mums were doing the same, but the kids still curse me for it!

They say, 'We can't believe you dressed us all the same, Mother!' And I have to defend myself, saying, 'Every girl used to be dressed the same, and every boy used to wear the same clothes, so it was normal!' But they just shake their heads at me in despair, embarrassed by our family photos!

At one point, though, someone, I think it was the mum-in-law, said I should let the girls grow their hair if they wanted to, and I agreed with her. Carol was the first one who chose to. I remember she decided to let it grow out, and she had this nice long blonde hair – and despite all my panic beforehand, luckily we didn't get overrun by nits!

Anyway, I remember one time when I was determined to take some time away from the pub. There was a protest march against a counsellor called Horace Cutler who was on the GLC – Greater London Council – and was in charge of housing. He had instructed that some council flats were to be pulled down in the area, and people weren't happy about it and came in The Rising Sun and asked us to join in a protest march. It was just round the corner from the pub, so I reckoned I would only be gone for an hour or so.

The kids were really young, but I took them along and they loved it. They couldn't walk for long, but there were open-topped lorries that the children and elderly people could sit on to keep up with the rest of the marchers.

We went down the road with hundreds of other people – I couldn't believe how many there were – chanting and marching, and singing a song that went like this:

'Cutler has only got one ball, the other is in the old town hall!'

I'm not sure if we had the impact we were intending but I actually quite enjoyed it, and at least it was a change from working in the pub. I think the kids were quite fascinated by the whole thing as well, and Stephen kept repeating the chants when we got home!

I'm not really a political person, though. In one way I'd like to be as it's politics that determines the way we live, but on the other hand I always wonder to myself what politicians really do. They promise one thing then they do something else. They couldn't care less half the time, at least that's how it feels.

But I've always made a point of voting. My husband was a real stickler for it, and I think that rubbed off on me. Nine times out of ten during our lives we voted Conservative, but then sometimes Labour too, depending on who was in power and whether they seemed to be promising anything particularly great.

I think it was in my head too that the Suffragettes

were a big thing in our area – although before my time, mind. Sylvia Pankhurst had fought a lot of her battles to get the vote for women from her headquarters in Bow Road. So there was still a bit of a sense in the local area of what they had achieved, and I felt somehow that I'd have been a bit disrespectful to her memory like, if I hadn't voted.

About a year after we moved into the pub I told my girls the story of Clara Grant. I didn't often spend time telling them stories from my own childhood, but for whatever reason this one time I told them how I always used to go down to her house of a Saturday when I was a child. Clara was a lovely kind old lady, who would put together packages filled with toys, marbles, hand-kerchiefs, pencils . . . anything a youngster would like to own. Then hundreds of kids would come from miles around and queue up at her house in Fern Street, off Devons Road, to get a 'farthing bundle', as they were called, off her. They got their name because each child handed over a farthing in exchange, which made them feel as though they had bought it rather than it being charity. But of course that was hardly any money, and Clara was doing it out of the goodness of her heart to help working-class people.

I explained to the girls how you had to fit under this special wooden arch that led into her house, which she had created to make sure only young children would be able to get a bundle.

Well, of course, they loved the idea of it – free toys as far as they were concerned! So they were all like, 'Take us down there, Mum!'

So I went, 'Come on then!' and one Saturday we went down there, me and four of the kids. June was too old by then and would have been too tall, so she decided to stay home.

Well, Clara Grant had died by then – she was an old lady in my memories of her as a child. She had died in 1949 at the age of eighty-two, but had been awarded an OBE for her charity work shortly before she died.

The nice volunteer ladies who had worked with her had decided to carry it on. So it was running nearly exactly the same as it had back when I was a child, in the same building on Fern Street, with the same archway to get under, although there were different ladies giving out the bundles and by then you had to give a penny per bundle now, rather than a farthing. Not that you could complain – it was still so cheap that it was more a gesture than a payment like.

Anyway, Susan, Carol, Stephen and Charlie all got in line, all excited, and waited their turn. There weren't the hundreds of children there had been in my day, but it was still busy enough. And I tell you, I felt a bit emotional as I remembered all my happy memories there from when I was young. Clara Grant was a very decent, kind woman. And I was back reliving my memories and seeing my children as excited as I used to be.

Well, anyway, they got to the front and, can you believe, Susan was too tall. She was a very tall girl for her age and you could see she and these other two girls near her were too big to fit under the arch, even before they tried, and despite all their best ducking and slouching efforts, it wasn't to be.

But the other others were more than happy with their bundles – and lucky for Susan, were happy to share!

Well, we only went down to visit Clara Grant's the once. We never really had another chance to go back as we didn't have the time. But I was glad I had shared the experience with the kids, and I know it made an impression on them – if I say the name 'Clara Grant' to them now, they know straightaway who I'm talking about and they start laughing as they remember that day.

The only sad bit of the story is that the bundles have now stopped. They continued until 1984, but then ended for whatever reason. The arch still exists, though – it is kept in the Fern Street Settlement, a charity for elderly people. I went and saw it recently and I'm so little that I could almost still fit under it!

As for actual holidays while we were in the pub, are you sure?! Not a hope in hell. As I say, a day off was a luxury, let alone a proper holiday. No, our poor caravan sat lonely while we were in the pub.

Charlie wasn't going on beanos no more either. Those were what you called days out, when a group of men would head off on a coach for the day, mostly to Southend. They would be loaded down with crates of beer and packed lunches, and would be well on their way to being drunk before they had even arrived at the coast! Then they would spend the day entertaining themselves at the fair or what have you with other people who were on beano outings as well.

Once we were in the pub, though, Charlie never got a chance to go on them – I think it was another thing that just became a casualty of us having no time.

In fact, the pub was putting a huge strain on us as a family, and not only in terms of how little time we all had to enjoy ourselves. It was the financial side of things that almost drove us to breaking point . . .

After we had been in the pub for about eighteen months, we started to have a real problem with the accounts. No matter how many times we did the maths at the end of the night, we always came up short. Oh, it was frustrating and drove Charlie wild. The arguments we used to have about it were out of this world.

We would spend hours reckoning up the money, but we were always a pound short, or sometimes even a fiver – and them days that was a lot of money. At first it was happening occasionally, and that would put Charlie in a right bad mood, but then it started happening nine nights out of ten and it began to drive him crazy.

Oh, the nights we sat there counting and recounting that money, checking every ha'penny, and it wouldn't add up. Sometimes it would just be that the amount was wrong, and other times it would be that there would be something, say a couple of packets of fags, not accounted for.

'You've given them too much change!' he'd shout at me. Or 'June must have done it, given them too much money back!'

'We've not!' I'd angrily defend us. 'We've given 'em the right money! You must've added it up wrong!'

And I even took to showing him the change I was giving customers to try and prove my innocence. I could feel him watching me more closely when I was counting out money, which made me feel awful and all anxious, as though my own husband didn't trust me.

'There are two packets of fags gone. Have you had them? Have you had them?!' he'd yell.

'No, we've not had them! Charl', it was nothing to do with us!'

'Well, where've they gone then? Someone's done it!'

Oh, and there'd be murder over whatever was missing. It was awful. We had so many rows over it – he'd go berserk, and I'd go to bed night after night and cry, cry, cry my eyes out. He would never apologize, though, as he could never be convinced that we were innocent. Until he got to the bottom of it, there was going to be no getting past it and he was forever going on about it.

I swear it's the closest I came to leaving Charlie, walking out on him, because he swore blind we were robbing him, and what wife is going to accept having her and her children called thieves?

But at the same time I could see why it was driving him crazy – a pound was a pound, and it was lot of money in them days. Not like today when people seem to throw money away on nothing. Besides, it was our own business, so for Charlie every penny counted and he wanted to get it right.

My husband was very cute on everything. He didn't even have to write it down, he had it all up in his brain, so he knew straight away when something wasn't right.

He was a businessman and he couldn't understand why things just weren't adding up. Something was definitely wrong.

In the run-up to Christmas 1969, this had been going on for a few months when something strange started to happen. Whenever I was behind the bar, the locals kept handing over presents. 'Would you give this to Juliette, please.' 'Give Juliette this wee gift as a thank-you for the last year,' and so on.

No presents for me and Charlie when we ran the pub, but all these gifts for our barmaid!

Well, I couldn't work it out, until finally a friend of ours who used to come in there regular every week pulled us to one side one night and asked to have a quiet word.

'If you want to know why Juliette is so popular, well, I've been watching her, and she's not taking money off some of the customers. She's giving them drinks for free without you knowing.

'Then other times she's taking more money out of the till than what she is putting in. Just thought you should know.'

And that's how we found out, and I was so, so upset. I'd really trusted Juliette, thought she did a good job, and got on with her as a friend. I felt right betrayed by her. It's strange we had never even suspected her, but I guess it was proof that people you trust really are still capable of dishonesty.

And Charlie, well, he was obviously not happy about it, so he told her she could work to the end of the week and then go. He wouldn't have gone to the police as Charlie just preferred to sort things out for himself, and he knew sadly it was always a risk with people you hired who were trusted with the pub's money. There was no row, she just accepted it – I guess it would have been hard for her to argue anyway.

I was right sorry to see her leave as she was a nice girl and had made my life easier behind the bar, but at the same I felt so let down.

And true enough, as soon as she went, we would reckon the money up at the end of the night and it would come up perfect to the penny, even the halfpenny of it all. Oh, it makes me mad to look back, but at least we had finally got to the bottom of it – and just in time to save our marriage! Not that Charlie ever apologized for accusing me and the kids, but I never expected him to, it wasn't his way. And actually, as it turned out, when it came to the kids, he wasn't that far from the truth! Because, just when we thought all our thieving woes were sorted out, it turned out they weren't . . .

From time to time we would realize we were short a crate of lemonade, or a box of crisps. Never alcohol, just soft drinks and food, but it was enough to make a dent in our profits.

My husband used to say to me, 'Those bleedin' cellar men! You wait till they come round here next week . . . they've fiddled me again! I'll give them what for 'cause they've lost me a case of this or that.'

Well, of course the poor delivery men, who always brought us everything we ordered, denied it, and Charlie checked the stock and it all seemed right. But again we were losing stuff. We couldn't get our heads around it.

Until one day when I was tidying upstairs and came across some little empty bottles and crisp packets hidden in the back of a cupboard. It turned out the kids had discovered the dumb waiter and had decided to put it to their own good use!

Little Charlie could just about fit inside it and, as the youngest, he was at the beck and call of all the others. So they were putting him in there and winding him down to the cellar, with instructions of what to bring back. And he'd get the crisps or lemonade or arrowroot biscuits and climb back in, and they'd wind him up again and have their own little feast upstairs. And we had never even noticed, even though it was going on for weeks and weeks. We were puzzling away downstairs, and those cheeky kids were getting the better of us upstairs. Having a right laugh at our expense no doubt! Oh, Charlie was a devil, a right little so and so. Although he is a good boy now!

I'm sure they thought they were being very funny and clever, but I tell ya, Big Charlie didn't! No, they got a right telling-off for that trick. But at least they kept their thieving hands to themselves after that!

SEVEN

On the Wrong Side of the Law

The one time Rex was allowed downstairs was closing-up time when we'd allow him free reign of the bar. As I say, people are always cautious of Alsatians, and I didn't try and change their opinions – because it was useful to me and Charlie when we wanted them to leave!

Rex was already growing fast and was turning into a huge beast of a dog. So at the end of the evening, if people were being a bit slow drinking up, we'd let Rex down the stairs. Then all he'd have to do was 'woof woof' and that was it, people understood that it was time for them to go. Suddenly empty pint glasses were handed over, the drinkers were out the door, and we were able to lock up! He was a good bouncer was Rex.

As for lock-ins, we didn't really go in for them much. Charlie might let the odd friend stay on, especially if he was in the mood for having another drink with him himself, but mostly as we had to get on with working out the money, we closed on time.

But one night in the summer of 1970 we decided to have a big after-hours party. It was someone's birthday, I forget whose, so we agreed to a lock-in, although they were called something different in them days – drink overs.

It was Charlie who agreed to it, but a bit after closing time, just as everything was getting well underway, there was a knock at the door, and when my husband opened it, two policemen walked in.

'What's going on here?' said the littler of the two chaps. He spoke in a very loud voice, maybe to make up for being so small. 'This is after the hours you are licensed to serve.'

Well, Charlie went for the friendly tactic, and started being all chatty with the copper. 'Ah look, I don't often do it, but it's a good friend's birthday so we're just relaxing with a few drinks. It would be good if you could just let us do it this one time.'

'Nope, no, I want everybody out of here,' he ordered.

Then Charlie went to the till and pulled out a note – I'm not sure how much – and passed it to the policeman. 'Take that, and it'd be great if you decide you'd never knocked on the door this evening.'

Well, that did not go down well.

'Don't you dare do that! Don't you dare try and bribe me!' he shouted. 'Everyone out of here now or there will be serious trouble!' and with that the two policemen stood there and waited until every last drinker was out, before they gave Charlie a final warning that he'd be nicked if we did it again.

Oh, we called him every name under the sun after he left – 'cocky little git' is maybe the only repeatable one of them! And that's what he got known as whenever we talked about that evening again. Really, what a bleedin' spoil sport.

As for Charlie, well, he just used to say, 'If I ever see that man again . . . '

I tried to keep the children out of the bar as often as I could, but it wasn't always possible and, in fact, they ended up down there quite a lot! I remember Stephen used to want to come down just to play his favourite game in the pub. I forget the name of it, but it was something the brewery had given us to keep in the bar. It was a bit like a tombola and I suppose it was the equivalent of having a fruit machine in the pub today. It was this big square block that sat on the bar, which had all these little holes in it. You would pay some small amount to have a go, and then you could push a pin in one of the holes and a little number would pop out. There were various prizes with numbers on, and if the number you made pop up matched the number on one of the prizes, you won it.

Well, the main prize this one time was a watch, and Stephen had his heart set on it. His dad had a few goes on it for him, but never won anything. Then one day one of the locals was playing it and got the number matching the watch, but what did he do? He gave it to Stephen. That was a proper nice gesture and you should have seen Stephen's face light up. He wore that watch all the time after that.

And then I could hardly stop June coming in the pub, could I, when at other times she was working in there as a little barmaid! So I made a deal with her once we had been in the bar for a year or two. If she could get all the other four into bed and asleep, then she could come downstairs of an evening.

So she would put her nightdress on over the top of her clothes and pretend she was getting ready with them all. Then she would get her two brothers off to bed and make sure they were asleep. She and her sisters slept in the same room together, in three single beds, and she had the middle one. They would all go off to bed at the same time and she would pretend she was sleeping until she knew they were asleep, then she'd creep out the room, all quiet like, nightdress would come off, and she'd come and join us downstairs!

She would then just sit and chat with us at the bar for a bit. The regulars would all talk to her as they knew her from behind the bar, and you could see she felt really grown-up being down there. Not that we would let her drink. No, a lemonade was the strongest June got! Every now and then I'd worry about her looking too young and get her to put on that eyeshadow, just in case anyone started questioning her age and her right to be in there. 'Make yourself look older, Juney, before you come down tonight,' I'd say, and sure enough she'd appear at the bar with green eyes.

As for entertaining the locals, we used to put on live music for a Friday, Saturday and Sunday, as that always went down well. It didn't have to be anything compli-cated – just a few tunes that got everyone in a weekend mood. We had a piano at the bar, and we hired this fella called Ginge to come and play it for us. I forget his real name, but obviously he was a ginger-haired chap. He'd come in and play whatever he was feeling in the mood for, or whatever old classics people requested, and he was really good. He'd play anything from Frank Sinatra's 'My Way', to 'The Entertainer' or 'Roll Out the Barrel' as the evening progressed.

Sometimes you'd even get people up and dancing –

a good ol' cockney knees-up! There wasn't too much space for it in the pub, but if the urge kicked in, every now and then people would start dancing and stamping around the place.

But mostly everyone would stay sitting down and just sing along with him, or other times one person would get up and sing properly. More often than not that was my Uncle Joe. He loved it. Occasionally he would take a turn on the piano too, although he was missing a finger. He had lost half the middle finger on his left hand and there was just a stump in its place. I think he lost it when he was in the army.

We had a dartboard in the pub as well, which would keep the locals entertained. People always liked a game of darts, and we ended up forming a men's team and a women's team. Of course, Charlie was on the men's team and I ended up on the women's one – although don't ask me how I got roped into that because I wasn't any good!

Most of the other pubs had darts teams too, and soon enough a tournament began so that once a week we played against each other. Either they would come to you or you would go to them, and they turned into quite the social occasion. My team generally lost as we were so bad – although once we had been in the pub a good couple of years and I finally got the hang of it, we managed to win a few times!

I enjoyed the matches when they were at our pub, and I used to do big platters of food – sandwiches and the like – and send them downstairs on the dumb waiter for everyone to eat while they played and drank.

But when it was in other pubs I wasn't so keen, and I'd make excuses not to go. Oh, I was terrible. But I had to do it really. I couldn't do nothing else because of the kids. On a normal night I'd be running up and down the stairs every five minutes, shouting, 'You all right?' and then running back down.

On the couple of occasions I did go to another pub to join the darts visits, we'd leave someone like Joe looking after the bar. But he couldn't keep an eye on the kids as well, so I spent the whole evening phoning through. 'You all right?' I'd ask June when she picked up, but all I'd hear was screaming and fighting and rowing. So I'd be beside myself, thinking that I needed to get back, and didn't enjoy one minute. Back in our pub, though, the tournaments were always good fun.

As you can tell, our lives were dominated by the pub. Even our nights of fun were spent playing darts with our punters. We didn't have time for anything else, and thankfully we always seemed to be fit and healthy enough to keep up the long hours the pub demanded from us. Charlie had never been one for getting sick. But from time to time he'd come down with a bit of a cough or a cold, mostly if he had been working 'specially long hours. When he felt one coming on, he'd just go, 'I've got a rotten cold, girl. Get me a barley wine.'

Oh, I'll never forget that drink. It's a strong ale, around 10 per cent, so around the same strength as wine but made from barley, hence the name. It has a really dark colour and smells awful, though. I never knew how anyone could drink it. But the other men would be the same – minute they felt something coming on, they'd be saying, 'Give us a barley wine, love.' Then they'd sit by the open fire – we had this proper nice old-fashioned open fire in The Rising Sun – and they'd have the wine in a glass or one of those old metal pint glasses. They'd put a poker into the fire until it was absolutely red hot, then they'd put it into their drink and you'd hear this 'shzzzzzzzzz' as the heat hit the wine. Then they'd drink it when it was lovely and hot. Oh, the things they used to do, it's unbelievable!

They always went and got drunk on it, and sure enough the next day their cold would be all gone – only to be replaced by a hangover!

No, Charlie's only problem was a duodenal ulcer – or stomach ulcer – that he'd had for years, but that had never really seemed to bother him. He would take Rennies and things like that from time to time, but the ulcer wasn't something that got him down or stopped him doing anything in life.

But then one day it took a turn for the worse. We were in the pub just like normal when he said he felt a bit weird and his stomach hurt, then he started bringing up blood. I can't remember if he actually fainted, but he felt like he was going to at least – and, to be honest, so did I looking at the blood! It was obvious he wasn't well, so we got him an ambulance and they took him to St Andrew's Hospital, just round the corner on Devons Road. It has since shut down and been turned into apartments, but back then it did the job well enough.

It turned out his ulcer had burst and he had a hernia, and he had to stay in hospital while they repaired it. Well, we couldn't just shut the pub up. No, I had to keep it open. But we had decided not to replace Juliette when we had fired her, partly as we had felt let down by her and didn't want to repeat the mistake, and partly to save money. So at this time I started to run The Rising Sun on my own – or at least as much as I could. There was no stopping Charlie, though, who was still doing his best to give out instructions from his bed! But it was scary being in charge, and it wasn't easy, I tell ya. But it was nice to see how much people rallied around.

The landlords and landladies at the other three corner pubs were a great help and really looked out for me.

They'd phone across, asking 'You all right, Pat? How's Charlie? Is there anything we can do for you? Do you want one of our bar people to come over and help you out for the day?' and all that like.

Oh, it was good of 'em, but that was the way it was back then – all of us helped each other out when we could.

Even the locals were wont to behave themselves a bit more around that time. I guess they could see how full my hands were, so they decided not to play up, you know. They'd leave when I asked them to, and check everything was going well. In a way they were quite protective of me, and it was nice to feel that so many people were there for me.

While Charlie was in hospital I had to learn how to do all the things he would normally do, and changing the barrels was one of the things I found the hardest. Oh, I tell ya, until I got a hang of it the beer used to go all over the place!

Charlie had shown June how to do it once 'cause she was interested in it all. She liked to watch him washing the pipes out and getting the cellar in working order. But she was still too young – and too small – to be lugging barrels around and taking responsibility for anything like that. She was helping me out in the bar still, and I tried to make it more official at the time. I asked the police for permission for her to stand behind the bar in case there was any trouble and she could call them up, and they agreed that was fine.

I also had some good help off my dad, and Uncle Joe, who used to come and change a barrel or stand behind the bar to help me serve. They were good at that time really, Dad and Joe. And they never expected money in return, although I'd give them a free pint or two.

They would look after the pub as well when I needed to run over to the hospital for visiting hours each evening. I'd say to Juney, 'Run over and get Uncle Joe,' when it was time, and she'd skip off over the car park and up to his flats. She'd knock and he'd tell her to wait, but she was too impatient and would always run back ahead of him.

I'd never think twice about sending her, even if it was dark by then, as although the East End could be tough in some ways, it wasn't threatening. I would never have worried that she'd have been attacked or raped or anything like that. Most likely the people she saw on her way she'd know anyway. And if not, everyone would still be looking out for her, looking out for each other. I'd be more scared today really. Unfortunately, I think that same community feel has long gone.

One character I was 'specially glad to have around at this time was Rex. Even if we all knew he was as soft as could be, others didn't, and as I've said, he was a fear-some creature by this point. So if there was ever any sign of trouble brewing, I'd say to Juney, 'Go and get Rex,' and we'd have him down behind the bar with us. He was a great deterrent.

And then, as if we weren't getting enough bad news, or struggling enough to cope, our poor ol' cleaning lady Winnie died. I don't remember the exact details of it, but I was sad about her. She was a nice kind lady, who had been there for most of our pub life.

After a couple of weeks in hospital, Charlie was given the all-clear and came out of St Andrew's. The doctors had operated on him to try and repair the lining of his stomach, which was damaged. But otherwise it seemed like he was fine, so they let him go with instructions to look after himself.

Now, I'm no doctor, but I am sure his drinking can only have contributed to causing the ulcer in the first place, so, of course, when he came out, you might have thought he would cut down. But, as always, Charlie did what Charlie wanted to do. I didn't even waste my breath telling him to stop the drinking, and as for any worries I had about it, I put them to the back of my mind.

EIGHT

Moving On

Between one thing and another, pub life was really starting to wear me down. Yes, there were good things about it, but there were a hell of a lot of bad things too. Charlie's illness had been stressful. I was also tired of not getting a minute to myself, and I kept feeling like I was neglecting the kids.

Things came to a bit of head at Christmas in 1970. Once again, me and Charlie had had the usual disagreement over whether we should open on Christmas Day, and, yet again, he had won. But when, as in previous years, I couldn't find the time to make Christmas dinner and the kids were just sat upstairs waiting, well, I just reached my limit.

'I am not staying in this pub another year, Charl'. I just won't! It's not fair or right on me or the kids.'

'OK, we'll be out soon,' he said.

But I had heard that before, and this time I wasn't standing it. 'It's me or the pub!' I just suddenly shouted, half crying and threatening him in a way that wasn't usual for me.

And you know what the cheeky git said? 'Go on then, pack your bags.' He wasn't the least bit scared by my threat. I was so frustrated, but had no intention of leaving at all. I had just hoped that it would at least shake him up. But once again he won. Or so he thought . . .

Because just a couple of weeks later I was picking up a crate of beer down in the cellar to take into the pub and, although Charlie was supposed to be taking it easy, he obviously felt he shouldn't be sitting back watching a woman do the heavy work.

So he went, 'Oh, for God's sake, give us 'em 'ere.' But as he snatched the crate off me, it burst the ulcer open again.

Oh, it was awful. He started bleeding again and was in so much pain, so we had to get him another ambulance. And we went through the whole process again of Charlie in hospital and me doing the best I could in the pub.

This time it was a longer process as well, as they couldn't risk it repeatedly happening. So he had a couple of operations before they could repair it, I suppose because the lining of his stomach was so damaged. It was quite involved, and at the finish they got something from America, like some sort of gauze that went around his stomach to hold it together.

Well, when he came out of hospital this time I said to him, 'I can't stand being in the pub much longer. It really is bringing me down. We've gotta get out.'

And my husband, well, I expected him to disagree, but he must have realized the same thing inside and known it was our time to move on 'cause he just went, 'Right, well, OK. We'll have to move then.'

And that was it. Just like that he started to look at places we could move to.

We had no set idea of where we wanted to move to, just a nicer area. We had saved a bit of money in the pub and decided we could buy our own place this time. Before the pub we had been in a council-owned terraced house that we had shared with his mum. Now we wanted our own house, and a detached one at that!

I remember him and Carol went and viewed some houses around Barking and Ilford as that was an area we kept hearing good things about. I know it was away from the world we knew in the East End, but we were ready for change, and I suppose it was a step up in the world.

They both came back all excited, chattering about

gardens and conservatories and the amount of space there was in the area. And we ended up buying a place they had seen in a road called Chudleigh Crescent in Ilford.

So after just over three years in the pub, we sold up and moved on. I can't remember who bought it – it wasn't anyone we knew – but I suppose it was the brewery who would have been responsible for sorting it out.

We didn't actually have a big leaving party or anything. We just told the locals one by one, and they would have a few drinks with us, and say, 'We can't believe you're going! Why are you? We'll miss you,' and all that. But we didn't have one big party.

I remember the day we moved. A little bit of me was sad to say goodbye to the pub, but mostly I was right glad to get out. Don't get me wrong, we had some really good days in The Rising Sun. A lot of my ideas of what life would be like in a pub before we moved there were wrong, and actually I think we did a really good job of running the place.

But the downsides were horrible and one of the biggest problems was, I think, that we just did it too early. I was thirty-five, Charlie was forty, and the kids were still too young. I couldn't handle everything I needed to be doing with them as well as all my duties in the pub, and I felt so guilty all the time that I wasn't being as good a mum as I wanted to be 'cause I plain just didn't have the time. If the kids had been a few years older, I think it would have been easier, but as it was, it just got too much. And I'll tell you what, it was only after moving and being able to spend proper time with the kids again did I realize how much they really didn't get to see their parents when they were in the pub.

Nowadays you might get people to work for you so that you could spend more time with your children, but that wasn't the way things were done back then.

The day we left the pub is the last day we ever set foot in there. We never went back for a visit. I wasn't really that fussed about it, and I don't think Charlie wanted to go back and see someone else in charge of his pub! It would have been too weird.

Shortly after we left, though, I remember bumping into someone from the area, and they told me that the new owner had opened up some of the upstairs as like a hotel, which I suppose if you were in the pub on your own, or as a couple, you could easily do as there was so much room. Then a few years later someone told me it had changed from that into a restaurant. I still never went back to have a look, though.

From what I understand, only the front of the pub is there now, preserved like, but the actual building behind it has changed – it is now flats, if I'm not wrong. Same goes for the other three pubs on the street. None of them are pubs any more – they've all been turned into different things.

But as I left for the final time that day, I can honestly say I had not one regret about going. My mind was already focused on the future. The pub was a chapter of our lives that had been good at times, but which ultimately I was glad to leave behind.

Looking back, I feel rightly embarrassed about the day we pulled up to our new house in Ilford in our big family estate car packed right to the roof. We must have been exactly like *The Beverly Hillbillies*.

We didn't have that much furniture as most of the stuff in the pub had been left by the landlord, so we had to leave the majority of it behind – apart from the latest three-piece suite! So we bought a lot of it new for this house. Although the one big thing we had taken from The Rising Sun was the portable bar from upstairs. There was no way Charlie was letting that stay behind, and setting it up in the living room of our new house was, I think, his way of not completely giving up his feeling of being landlord!

What we did have, though, was a rabble of children and animals . . . As we pulled up and climbed out, all the kids were excited and noisy and pushing into each other, and Rex was running around and barking as he picked up on the excitement. I can still picture it. One of the kids was holding the canary cage, another the goldfish bowl . . . I often look back now and think 'Oh my God!'

I am sure there must have been some serious curtain-twitching going on that day as the neighbours saw us arrive and wondered what the hell the street was in for!

But that aside, it was a great feeling to walk through the front door of our new house, and know this was our new life beginning – we now owned this lovely place!

We unloaded all our belongings and bags, and the little furniture we had, and Charlie left me and the kids and a friend of June's at the house while he went back to the pub to lock it up and finish off any last bits.

Well, in the end it got so late that Charlie decided to stay at the pub for one last night, and me and the kids were in the new house on our own. They spent the first night watching *Dracula* on television and managed to frighten the life out of themselves. But I was exhausted and needed my bed that night, so I left them to it!

It was a strange feeling waking up for the first time in our new home at number 27 Chudleigh Crescent. When I opened my eyes, I had no idea where I was, but then the sound of the kids already up and about, excitedly exploring their new home, made me remember.

The house was on a right posh and proper horse-shoe-shaped road on the border of Barking and Ilford, made up of about fifty or sixty detached houses. We paid £5,500 for our three-bedroomed house, and by the time you took off whatever money we had saved from the pub, our mortgage repayments worked out at £10 a week.

Some of the houses had garages, although we didn't, but Charlie as good as treated the space on the road outside our house as though it was ours! If anyone put a car outside our place, he'd be out there in a flash. 'Oi, move your car. You can't leave it there!' He wouldn't have anybody other than us park their car out there.

It wasn't easy getting set up in the beginning. As I said, I was buying all new furniture from scratch really, so we had nothing for a while. I remember for the first week we were literally without anything. I still have an image in my head of making the kids' dinners, and them sitting with it on their laps on the stairs as we had nothing else for them to sit on! But bit by bit I started to get furniture together.

At the same time, though, Charlie got stuck straight into redesigning the house to make it exactly as he wanted. It had been older people in it before us and they had been in it for years and still had all the old fireplaces in each room. But Charlie decided he wanted them all taken out and replaced with proper heating, so as they were removed one by one, the house was rightly turned upside down and we seemed to be forever up to our necks in muck and dirt. But it was good in the end and gave me a chance to get new carpets fitted at the same time.

Anyway, as I said, with all the curtain-twitching on our arrival, I think there were plenty of people who didn't want us in that street when we first moved in to Chudleigh Crescent.

Some of the people who lived down the road actually helped build those houses in the 1920s, and it was them in particular who were quite obvious about not wanting us there. It sounds strange now, but back then we were almost like foreigners moving to a new country – all the locals were suspicious of us! They were like these very posh, selective sort of people, and I think they viewed us as cockney rabble, a mob of East Enders come to ruin the image of their area. Oh, the shock of a woman with five kids ruining the peace! I'm sure there was all kinds of gossip about us when we first arrived there.

And almost instantly, just to prove them right, Charlie had a falling out with a chap down the road – although I have to say, I definitely thought my husband was in the right.

Out of the children, it was Stephen who liked taking

Rex for a walk the most. He enjoyed spending time with him and they probably had the closest bond. But you have to remember, Stephen was still young, about eight, and by this time Rex was a big dog. So we used to joke that it was the other way around – most of the time Rex was taking him for a walk. Except sometimes that really wasn't a joke. There was one day when poor Stephen was walking along the street with him on a lead when Rex spotted another dog and decided to run after it. He literally dragged Stephen along the pavement while he clung on desperately to the lead, all the while burning his chest on the ground. Ouch, poor lad!

But it wasn't that incident that made Charlie fall out with the bloke down the street. No, it was when Stephen was walking Rex along one day, and again he spotted another dog and barked at it. Well, some bloke – I suppose he owned the other dog – kicked Rex. Stephen was too young to really do anything about it, but he came home all upset and told Charlie about it. And my husband being my husband, there was no chance he was going to let that go. So he went down the road, found the bloke and gave him a kicking instead!

'Don't you ever kick my dog again or I'll kick you all the way down the street next time!' he told him. Oh, I tell you, he knew how to hold his own did Charlie and no one was going to go round kicking our family and getting away with it. 'Cause that is what it was – Rex was part of our family.

Well, it was around this time that we were politely asked to piss off back to the East End – and I mean that literally!

The two boys were out playing on their bikes in the road one day, and I dunno what it was they did exactly but a lady up at the other end of the street came out and had a go at them. When they came back in for their dinner, they told me how she had said, 'Piss off back to where you're from! You're a bleedin' nuisance, your family!' I was so shocked by that. Twenty miles from our home in the East End, and you'd think we had gone to the other side of the world the way people were reacting.

Another neighbour who was unimpressed by our arrival lived in this big corner house with a huge great fence around the garden. Stephen and a couple of other local lads kept slinging Little Charlie over the fence and watching him scramble back out. Once, though, the old guy came out of his house and caught him and brought him back to our house, and when Big Charlie opened the door to see what was going on, the old man gave Little Charlie a cuff round the earhole and said, 'He's been climbing in my garden again!' As ever, there was plenty of curtain-twitching that day, I tell you . . . though maybe luckily for Little Charlie. For just as my husband was about to give him a hiding too, another neighbour across the road, Georgie Bates, came across and told him, 'It weren't Charlie's fault. It was Stephen and those other lads flinging him in there.'

So that was it. Stephen got the clap round the ear instead, and the other local lads got chased down the road by my husband.

How to make yourself the popular new neighbours!

And if all that hassle wasn't enough, there was another person who bothered me in our new life in Chudleigh Crescent. A neighbour just across the road made me feel right uncomfortable about living there. He was this small man who just seemed to be watching me all the time. Every time I went in or out of the house, just to take the kids to school or to nip out to the shops, I'd feel someone's eyes on me. I'd look up and this fella'd be standing in his doorway watching me.

Well, after about a week of it, I couldn't take no more and said to Charlie, 'There's a fella across the road and he's driving me up the wall, I'm not kidding you. He's always watching me and it's really making me feel all weird.'

'What? Where?' he asked, all protective and angry like. Then he went quiet for a bit. I realized I'd been stupid to open my mouth as I could see the rage in his eyes, and I thought to myself, 'Oh no, I'm going to have a punch-up on my hands and now even more of the neighbours are gonna be against us!'

And sure enough, a little while afterwards he headed for the door.

'Charl', where you goin'?' I asked, all afraid.

'Won't be a minute,' was the gruff reply I got, and off he headed, his jaw all tight like, and a determined look on his face.

I was all in a panic and ran to my front-room window to see Charlie striding across the road. Well, I was absolutely shaking from head to foot, so I decided to make a cup of tea to try to calm my nerves, but even that didn't help and I ended up splashing the hot water about everywhere.

He was gone a quarter of an hour, half an hour, and still no sign. After nearly an hour I'd just started to steady myself to go across the road and see what was happening when he came back. And a very different Charlie he was to the one who'd walked out the door. He was smiling away, and just sauntered into the house as though everything in the world was great.

'You're never going to guess who that was over there,' he went.

'No, who is it then?'

'Remember the copper that nearly nicked me for

having the lock-in at the pub, who I tried to bribe, but he was having none of it?'

'Yeah . . .'

'It's him! If he was staring so much, it is 'cause he was studying you, trying to work out if we were the same couple, 'cause he was sure he recognized us. And you know what? He's actually not a bad fella.'

'Well, what a small world,' I said, laughing with relief. 'At least I don't have to worry that there is some dirty old man living opposite now!'

Turns out he had apologized to Charlie as well for ruining our lock-in, but blamed it on the guy he was with. He told Charlie, 'You know what, if I hadn't had the other chap with me, I'd have said forget it and let you get on with your party. But I couldn't be seen in front of my workmate not to be doing the proper thing. So I couldn't do anything else like, other than make you shut it down. Very sorry about that.'

And, well, I soon got talking to him too, and his wife, and although I forget their names now, they really were a lovely couple and we became good friends after that. Not at all how I had imagined him to be that night in the pub when we were calling him every name under the sun!

Other people started to come round to us as well, and even the woman who had told the two boys that we should piss off back to the East End became friendly with us. Funnily enough, when we got talking to a lot of them, it turned out they were from much worse areas than ours. Obviously it was just our *Beverly Hillbillies* arrival that had left an impression!

Our immediate neighbours on one side were a couple called Mr and Mrs Watts. They were a lovely elderly couple who we got on really well with. I was always friendly with her and we were forever in and out of each other's houses. They were really relaxed and never complained about anything.

The neighbour on the other side was a different story, however . . . She was an elderly lady who lived on her own, and one day soon after we had moved in she stopped me and said, 'Excuse me, but could you please not hang your washing out on certain days.'

And I was thinking, erm, hang on, I have a husband and five kids, I need to hang out washing most days if I am to keep them clean! And there weren't tumble dryers in those days. But I was trying to be friendly, so I nodded and said I was sure I could fit round her, but asked what her reasoning was.

So she gave me a list of days, and told me, 'These are the days I have my friends over for coffees, and I think it is a bit unsightly for them to have to look at washing when they are round.'

OK, right . . . So from then on, I tried desperately to try and fit my washing around her social life, and I'd be dashing out on certain days to get it in before her friends got round. But it obviously wasn't good enough because she moved a bit after! And then a new couple moved in – he was yet another policeman, can you believe, called Ted, and his wife Shirley, who luckily turned out to be a nice pair.

So bit by bit, despite the wars with the neighbours, we began to settle in to our new life in Ilford, and it wasn't long before we felt as though we'd been there for years and our time in The Rising Sun began to feel like a distant memory.

NINE

High Days and Holidays

When we moved to Ilford it was Spring 1971 and the kids all started at school immediately. Carol, who was ten by then, Stephen, who was eight, and Charlie, who was seven, were at South Park Primary School, about half a mile away, on Water Lane.

The boys settled in quite well, as did the two older girls, but Carol wasn't so happy about it. Despite normally being a very confident and outgoing girl, she suffered a bit with the move and became very clingy to me. So she was quite distressed at first about going to a new school. I had to convince her to go each day, and we came to an agreement that she could come home at lunchtime rather than staying to eat in the school dining room. Being able to come home halfway through the day seemed to reassure her a bit.

She also started gymnastics classes, which she seemed

to love, and actually she was very good and ended up competing in it. She used to say she would have liked to have been in the circus, which I liked to think might have been in her blood. My mother's maiden name was Chipperfield and her family were part of the famous Chipperfield Circus, so maybe this was Carol just being true to her roots! She was also a good little swimmer, and went to classes and swam for a club in competitions as well.

I also started sending the kids to Sunday school at church each week. I think it did them no harm at all – in fact, it did them plenty of good and they had a lovely lady teaching them. It was a good way for them to learn good manners and morals, and it kept them busy on a Sunday too.

I'd go sometimes as well, though mostly I had work to do in the house or was busy preparing the Sunday dinner, while Charlie would be off having a drink and making friends over his pint.

The only problem with Sunday school was the obsession Carol developed with the piano in the church. She decided she wanted to learn to play the piano and wanted to buy one, but she didn't want any old instrument – no, it specifically had to be the one in the church. She came home one day and told me she had put her name down on the list to buy it, and she even told the priest she had saved up all her money to buy it. Of course she hadn't, but it didn't stop her trying. I told her in no uncertain terms that she couldn't have it as it would have taken up too much space, and it seemed like a waste of money – knowing Carol she would grow tired of it after a couple of months. In the end we bought her a little tiny thing to play at home, but she wasn't impressed, and after that, true enough as we expected, she lost interest and that phase went out the window.

Meantime, June, who was fourteen, and Susan, who was twelve, were at Mayfield Girls' School in Chadwell Heath. Not that June was making any more of a habit of going to school here than she did back in Bow. We made her walk together with Susan, but more often than not Susan would come home with tales of how June had skipped school once she was out of sight.

One time her attempt to miss school went a bit wrong, though. She had gone home and was upstairs when Susan got home. Susan heard June moving around and, as she thought no one was supposed to be home, called the police, thinking it was a burglar! I came home to find the police at the house checking out this so-called burglar. That was an embarrassing day.

June stuck out school for another year and then left at the first opportunity, getting a full-time job in a hair-dressing salon near home.

As for me and Charlie, we were enjoying having a bit more free time, although as soon as we had decided we were leaving the pub, Charlie figured that his next move would be to run a shop, so was on the lookout for a suitable place. I think he thought he would get the social aspect of the pub, and the selling bit, which he enjoyed, but without such long hours. He always liked having his own business as well rather than working for a big company or organization 'cause that way how much you earned was determined by how hard you worked – and he was always willing to work very hard.

Meantime, I was glad not to be working. I wanted the time to get our new house set up like a proper home, the kids settled in, and do some of the jobs I had barely had a minute to do in the pub, like cleaning and making proper family meals. In fact, cooking was something I loved doing during that time!

Some food was the same as what you might eat today, and other times it was different. Don't get me wrong, you can still buy it all – it's just that tastes change, and people today would turn their noses up at some of the meals I served then. Like stewed or jellied eels, which, as ever, were one of our favourites. I have always believed in buying the eels live and then killing them myself just before I cook them, so they are as fresh as possible. And

I remember the kids loved playing with them while they were still alive and wriggling.

I'd get them from the fishmonger's and I'd feel them moving about in my bag on the way home, then I'd lay them out on the draining board once I got indoors. I remember the kids always coming over and picking them up, sliding them through their hands because they were so slimy. They were fascinated by them. Then I'd get out the knife – chop, chop! – and they'd be in the pan.

Other times we would have pigs' trotters. I wouldn't eat them now, but back then you were glad enough to eat them. It was something everyone enjoyed. People used to say, 'Oh, the ol' pig trotter! Munch, munch, munch!' You'd hold on to 'em by the two little trotters while you ate the rest.

And then there was sheep's brain . . . You'd serve that up on toast and it was lovely. Why shouldn't you eat it? Make use of all the bits. People say, 'Oh, offal,' nowadays and turn their noses up at it, but things like liver, kidney, heart . . . it's all perfectly edible. You just got to get over being squeamish 'cause you don't know what you are missing!

As for sheep's heart, oh, that is beautiful. I used to cut one open and take the valves out, put in stuffing that I had made from breadcrumbs and what have you, and then tie it closed again with a piece of string, put it in the oven for a while, and there you go – a lovely, tasty piece of meat.

Those kinds of foods seem to have disappeared now, although someone told me recently they are making a comeback in gourmet cooking! So I bet you find that kind of food being served up in London's top restaurants, marketed as a delicacy or what have you. I bet it's on The Ivy's menu and Gordon Ramsay's serving it in his restaurants!

It's funny how meats go in and out of fashion, and how it affects the price of some of them. Take a breast of lamb, for instance. That used to be just an ordinary dinner for our family. I'd buy five breasts of lamb for half a crown, but have you seen the price of them now? They were a cheap option then, but now they are a delicacy and so expensive. Innit weird how these things change?

I couldn't half get a few meals out of my five pieces of meat as well. I'd get them home and bone them, then I would put three to one side and just use the two for a Sunday dinner. I'd make stuffing – a whole load, to make the dish look like more than it was – and then I'd stuff it into the lamb breasts and roll them up. They'd look huge and would do the lot of us for our meal.

Then the other three I would make into a stew. I'd add just about anything that was going – loads of carrots, onions, the cat, socks that were lying around . . . ! At least that's how it felt at times. Anything I could find I'd chuck in – you name it, it was in a Pat stew at some point. I would chuck it all in and that would do me, Charlie and all the kids for a couple of days.

So see what I mean? Honest to God, I could get a good few meals for half a crown in them days if I used my head.

I also liked to make a good Sunday lunch, always served at 3 p.m. on the dot. That gave my husband a chance to go down the pub for a few drinks, and then head back and know his dinner would be ready.

Then later on for teatime I would do a mix of seafood, like winkles and cockles and prawns. I would get half a pint of that lot off the fishmonger who came round in his van doing deliveries on a Sunday morning, or from the fish stalls that opened up outside the pubs on a Sunday. Back then, near enough every pub in the East End and Essex had a fish stall outside it, although I know today you only really get one or two here and there.

After the pub on Sunday a lot of the men would go home, eat their dinner, then have a nap, and then they'd eat the cockles, winkles and shellfish of an evening when they woke up. That's what always happened in our house too. After I had got the seafood from the delivery man or the stall, I would shell it all and wash it, then put it in a big bowl with vinegar and salt and pepper. And when it was the evening and everyone was getting hungry again, I would put it out with a nice loaf of bread, and everyone would make their own sandwiches. It was lovely.

It has become harder and harder to find anywhere that sells decent seafood, though. The best is probably down at Southend, where there is a place called the Cockle Sheds. They specialize in seafood that has just been brought in fresh, so buying it down there is good.

But although Southend is still in Essex, it is about thirty miles from Ilford, so we couldn't get food from there normally. That was just if we went there for a day out. Our lot would leap on the train on a Sunday morning any time of year, and go down there for the day. It was just 50p on the train at the time and they would go to the Cockle Sheds and bring back big bags of the shellfish as well as getting their fill while they were there. Or sometimes we would all go down as a family.

It is still there today and sometimes me and Carol go down in the summer when it's a lovely day. It is one of those last-minute things you decide to do. 'It's sunny – it's a Cockle Sheds day!' we sometimes say, then off we go.

And now you get a platter, like a square plate that is divided up with little squares on it, each with a different seafood in it. Winkles in one lot, prawns in another, cockles in another, or whatever you want. Gorgeous!

As we had not been able to have many days out, if any, during our time at the pub, I was determined that that would change, so I always loved our trips to Southend. But one day here and there wasn't enough – we needed a holiday.

We still had our caravan at Leysdown on the Isle of Sheppey and, as I used to say to Charlie, I lived and died there. So as soon as we were out of the pub, going down there for a break was top on my list of things to do.

Despite the years of not going, Charlie of course still remembered the route perfectly. And as soon as we pulled up at our old caravan, I felt myself unwinding – it was like the place was linked in my mind with happy stress-free times. We had a lovely week there – going for walks, sitting, relaxing and talking, eating fresh seafood. And that was the start of regular visits for us again. I loved staying there, and more often than not our family and friends would come down there too.

We'd all squeeze into different caravans, or some-times we would make tents by putting up sheets between two cars – it was all just great fun. Our caravan had wheels but was static, so we couldn't drive it around or anything. We tried renting it out once when we weren't there, but when we did go back they had left it in such a state with stains and mess everywhere that we didn't do it again. So it sat empty when we weren't there – all the more reason for us to go down more often I used to say!

Some of my favourite memories over the years as the children were growing up were from there. Like the time when Susan was ever so young, only like three or something, and we were walking along the beach, and I remember she was wearing these great big wellie boots that were about five sizes too big for her that we'd borrowed as she didn't have any of her own. They were ridiculous. She was clumping along, and could hardly walk at all.

But one minute she was next to us, and the next . . . well, we'd lost her. We started running along the beach, calling out her name, but there was no answer. Oh, we started going berserk, panicking 'cause we thought she was in the water and we were going to find her drowned. Well, all these people started helping us look, and word went up and down the beach about this missing girl. Then someone called the police, and when they arrived I suppose I was a bit hysterical, 'cause the only way I could think to describe her by was these bleedin' great wellies.

Then all of a sudden someone hollered out, 'I think

Sheppey after we had fallen in love with the place on our honeymoon. On that trip, back when we still were living in Canning Town, we had rented one, but after that, with it becoming so special to us, we decided to buy our own. It was a real old gypsy-style caravan, with two doors, that cost us £90 – which may I say was a lot of money at the time! We had made good use of the caravan until we moved into the pub. Then we rarely had a moment to get any time off, so heading down there, even for a weekend visit, was a no go.

But later, when we had been in Ilford for a year or so, Charlie came into a bit of money and we upgraded! I think he won the money, although I forget the details. It wouldn't have been because of betting or anything like that, though. He wasn't a gambling man – in fact, he was quite against it. He saw it as a waste of money, because he was so good with money and knew the odds were always against you. He'd never even have a quick flutter on the horses or anything, which I've always thought was very good of him.

But anyway, this time he said, 'I'm gonna get a new caravan with this cash.' I thought he was daft and was perfectly happy with the one we had, so I said, 'Why waste money on a caravan?' But, of course, he had his mind made up, so he went for it and bought a lovely modern BK Bluebird, which, despite my fears, I completely fell in love with the first time we stayed in it, and was very happy he had invested in it! There was just so much space, and it felt clean, and everything was well thought out so that it all fitted in the right places. It felt like it was a real step up from the old caravan. We had some great trips down to stay there, and I was almost as at home in the Bluebird, as I was in my own house!

TEN

Dinner's Served!

Even though I was settling in to Essex life, I did miss the East End and all our family over there. I know Essex and the East End seem just down the road from each other by today's standards, but back then, given I'd pretty much been able to walk to see those closest to me in just a few minutes, being eight miles down the road was quite a shock. Essex seemed like another world!

So I was pleased whenever any of our family from the East End came out to visit. Sometimes we would visit them, but more often than not they would come to us as we had the bigger house so it was easier for us to have people to stay. Charlie would go and pick up whoever was coming over on a Saturday while I went in to Barking town centre to do some shopping with the kids.

In the beginning, before I went out shopping, Charlie would say, 'Well, what do you want to get?' I would make a long list and he would take a look, then say, 'Come on, let's go and get it then.' But it wasn't long before the novelty of shopping wore off for him and he'd say he couldn't be bothered, using the excuse of getting the relatives to get out of it. So he would give me the money instead for what we needed and off I would go with the kids.

Charlie still looked after all the money – that was very much his role – and when we were out he would pay for everything. If I was going out somewhere and needed some cash, I would ask him for it. It wasn't that he was being controlling – he never really said no – it was more just that it made sense for one person to look after that side of things, and he was best at it.

We never had credit cards as my husband didn't believe in them. He'd say, 'What do we want a credit card for? Whatever you want, pay for it straight away. Once you have one, you won't stop, so never get anything on the tic or you will end up in debt.' And actually I think he was right. We wouldn't have done so well with saving if we had behaved like that. It feels like people today use credit cards to buy what they want without thinking about whether they can afford it.

Anyhow, the kids always enjoyed the trip to the market in Barking where I would get my supplies, although their favourite was the broken biscuit stall. I used to go there and get this big box of all these bits of biscuits that were broken – all different sorts that I guess were like factory rejects, so they were cheaper than normal biscuits. Although if you were lucky you would still find some whole ones in there! The kids would be more than happy munching their way through them.

Then I would go to the butcher's to get the meat for the weekend, and if the kids were hungry there, I'd treat them to pease pudding and saveloys.

Pease pudding is a kind of mushed-up mix of yellow split peas, spices and ham, and it would come in cellophane, wrapped kind of like a bag of chips. Saveloys are like these bright red spicy sausages and they would dip the sausages in the pease pudding and eat them that way. The kids loved them so it would keep them quiet for a while, and fill them up until dinner time.

The children were always disappointed that there was never a monkey in the Barking market, though. Back in the East End, say in Petticoat Lane or up in Bethnal Green, you would often find a monkey, which people would pay to have their photo taken with. Generally they were dressed up, usually in baby clothes, and it always caused quite a stir. I think they probably came from one of the ships that arrived in at the docks, brought back by a sailor. Mostly, though, you didn't see them in Essex. In the East End you would get them in some of the pubs too – they would have a pet monkey in there as a bit of an attraction – but we never had one in The Rising Sun!

While I was in Barking I would also get my supply of 'forget-me-nots', our nickname for condoms. Back when I had lived in the East End, I'd had to buy these off a lady in Rathbone Market, called Mrs Winky, who ran the ribbon stall. You'd give her a wink and half a crown while buying something else, and she'd hand over a condom that she pulled from out of her apron. She'd do it all subtle like, wrapping it in whatever you were buying and slipping it straight into your bag. Contraception back then was always very hush hush. Even though everyone needed it, no one was supposed to admit it or discuss it. But by the time we were in Barking, it had become less of an undercover mission to get hold of them – the chemist had started supplying them. Boring, I know!

Then after we'd done all of our shopping, we would come back home to find one relative or another over for a visit. Sometimes Charlie's sister Mary and her husband George would come over. They had three kids that ours were friendly with – two boys, Ronnie and Georgie, and a girl, Linda, and the lot of them used to go off and play together while us adults caught up. They lived in Beckton High Road, and although they hadn't come in the pub that much, we had still stayed close. At the time we were a really tight family.

The kids loved playing around with their Uncle George. They always used to find it 'specially funny when he made them jump with his lump. George had some illness, I forget what, that caused this big bobbly-looking growth on his neck. But being a typical joker, he used to deny it was an illness that caused it – instead he always used to tell everyone he had been bitten by a camel! It was an awful-looking thing, and he'd always wind them up and say, 'Go on, touch it. Feel it. You ain't scared of it, are you?' and he'd convince them to reach up and touch it. Then just as they did he'd suddenly turn fierce and swoop at them pretending to bite them. It was only silly games like that, but they loved it and giggled for ages after. He was a jolly proper East End character was George.

Dad started coming over quite a lot at weekends too. He was retired now from his painting and decorating job, so was keen to spend as much time as possible with the family and he really warmed to the granddad role – I liked seeing him relaxed and enjoying spending time playing with the kids.

Then, of course, Uncle Joe would come over too, but he got himself a new girlfriend around this time . . . Can you believe, he started seeing Charlie's mum!

Charlie and his mum had always been close, and when we first married, we lived with her for thirteen years in Canning Town before we moved to the pub. She was a big character – and a big lady – and was always very popular with the men. Her last husband – her second or third, I'm not sure – had been a seaman called Sam Rowlinson, but he died around the time we were in the pub so she started coming in there, and she and Joe always got on well. They would sit together and have a laugh and a drink, and as they both had a similar sharp sense of humour they could spend hours amusing each other.

And before we knew it, well, she started going home with him sometimes, and other times he would go home with her, and it turned out they were dating and seeing each other. Then eventually she gave up her place and moved in with him. It was more of a friendship thing than anything else really, though. In my mind they were too old to be doing anything sexual, and it was more just the company they gave each other.

Charlie's mum was getting bigger and bigger at that time – if I'm honest, I've never seen anything like her bust in those days. It must have been about sixty-eight inches. And she was having a bit of trouble walking by this time, as her diabetes was getting worse and causing pains in her leg. But nevertheless she kept going, and she enjoyed coming to stay with us. She was especially fond of Carol – she thought she was a wonderful, diamond little girl.

June she was less fond of, partly I think 'cause she expected her as the eldest to help her, but June wasn't so keen.

Whenever she came to stay, we would give her June's bed. The girls slept in bunk beds in their room, and June would have to give up her bottom bunk and get in with one of the other girls. But the problem was that, because of her diabetes, she needed to get up to go to the toilet a lot in the night, and thanks to her bad leg and the pains she was getting in it, she couldn't get out of bed by herself. So when she needed to go, she would call out to June.

And poor June soon got tired of being woken every hour to help her up, so started pretending she couldn't hear her. Later she told us the mum-in-law had lain below getting more and more mad at her, and eventually hissed, 'June, if you don't get out of that bed this very minute, when you do, I'm gonna hit ya!' Oh, she was mad at her. Poor June!

June wasn't the only one who wasn't getting enough sleep, though. Despite my intention to stay 'unemployed' and focused on my family and home life for a while, it didn't take long before I was juggling my fair share of jobs – of course!

As always in those days, although we had a bit of money together by this stage, you could never be sure when things would fall down around you, so it seemed brash to turn down any chance to make some money. And when an opportunity arises, well, sometimes you just have to take it.

The first job came about thanks to my daughter Carol. As I said, she wasn't keen on her new school and refused to stay there for lunch, so would come home every day instead. She was really clingy at the time, and even though I tried to get her to stay for the school dinners, she wasn't having any of it and would just say she couldn't. So instead I would prepare her a little sand-wich at home each day, but woe betide me if I wasn't there to serve it up! There was one time when I wasn't there – I had to do some errand or another – but I had still left her food out as always. Well, she was so put out by my absence that I came home to find her lying on the floor with tomato ketchup squirted all over herself, trying to pretend she had been killed to make me feel guilty! I'll never forget that. She was so dramatic – and still is!

But one day less than a month after she had been at her new school, she came home and said, 'Mum, they want a dinner lady in school and I put my hand up and said, "My mum can cook," so I think you should do the job.'

'Thanks very much!' I said, and just laughed it off.

But anyhow, next thing I knew I got a phone call from the school asking me to call in to see the headmistress when I picked the kids up the next day. So I went in to her and she said they wanted someone to help out in the kitchen, and asked me if I was interested. She said it was only for a couple of hours a day. It had felt like I had been working a twenty-four-hour day in the pub, so I couldn't see the harm in just a few hours a day. After all, the extra money would come in handy.

She sent me to see the cook and have a chat with her, and she said it was mostly washing-up I would be doing and that it was only for a few weeks as a lot of people were going on holiday, and they needed extra help. They were a nice enough bunch of women and the hours would fit well around when the kids were at school, so I agreed to it and started the following Monday.

So there I was at the sink, washing up. I had to wear a kind of rubber pinny to protect my clothes, and spent three hours each day sterilizing dishes, tins, pots, etc., and then drying and gathering them up, ready for use the next day. I was working from 11.30 a.m. to 2.30 p.m. five days a week, and the wage was £3.80 a week.

But after the agreed few weeks were up and I was due to leave, the cook called me over for a chat and said she wanted help with what she was doing, and if I didn't want to leave, I could carry on by helping her with the food preparation. So I said I didn't mind helping her out. I was secretly really pleased to be asked, as I was enjoying the daily chat with the other women, and it was a compliment to be asked to stay. I became the second cook, after her, and got a brand new uniform to replace my rubber pinny – it was a white overall and a white hat, with a net that came down from the back of it to cover your hair.

I remember in my first week of cooking the school dinners she said to me, 'You're really good, ain't ya?!' And I was like, 'Well, I cooked for my dad and brother for most of my early life, then I've been feeding a husband and five kids for years, and then the pub . . . So I have had plenty of practice!'

Every day we were cooking meals for the whole school, and the children would pay 10 pence a dinner. And they really were lovely meals, if I say so myself! Proper dinners, not like a lot of the ready-meal type stuff they seem to have today. We did rolls of beef, legs of lamb, whole chickens or pies, with roast or mashed pota-toes, all prepared by hand and really fresh. No frozen chicken nuggets or pizza – nothing like that. Jamie Oliver would have been happy with our kitchen if he had been around to visit it back in the seventies!

We were told each Friday what the menu was to be for the following week, and the food was delivered for us. What we made changed each week, apart from Fish Friday. Every Friday without fail we served battered fish with potatoes of some kind. Any kid who didn't like it had the option of fish fingers instead and that was it. So it was an easy day for us! Definitely the least preparation of all the days.

As for sweets, these were 5 pence extra and were good hearty puddings. We made fruit or apple pie, chocolate pudding or sponge cake, and they were pretty much always served with custard or chocolate custard. And there was always a race to see who could get the skin on the top – you either love it or hate it!

I would help out serving the food to the children too, including to my own kids. Because now that I was at the school, of course Carol had decided she would stay there for lunch after all. Not that things were much better there – if she couldn't come behind the counter to see me, which she wasn't allowed to do as I was working, she would start crying all over again! But I just used to wave to her and try and reassure her that way, then get on with my job.

Other times I would look out the window after lunch

to see if she was doing country dancing in the playground with the other children, but every time I did I would find her looking up at the window, waiting to see me and be reassured. It was hard as a mum to see her being so unusually shy. But thankfully it didn't last long, and she soon settled in and went back to the old confident Carol.

As for the boys, they were at the school too and settled in there much more easily. Stephen just quietly got on with his studies and with the other kids, but as for Charlie, although he had settled in fine, he wasn't quite so well behaved . . .

I used to dread walking through the school hall sometimes, 'cause more often than not I would see him in there in trouble. When he had been naughty, he had to stand in there facing the wall. I'd say, 'Charlie! What's happened now?' in whichever voice I was trying at the time to get through to him – sometimes angry, sometimes disappointed.

'Well,' he'd start, 'it was that teacher!' or 'it wasn't my fault, it was his!' That was the way with Charlie – it was never his fault. It was never ever him! It was always someone else that done it.

But he did his crimes with such a cheeky charm and a twinkle in his eye that it was like it pained the teachers to punish him. They used to say to me, 'He is very naughty, but we do love him!'

I think his biggest problem was chattering. He couldn't keep quiet and was always talking to some person or another.

And, of course, he would get the cane sometimes, as would Stephen, although he always claimed he was innocent too – obviously! But I was more likely to believe Stephen. He was always such a good boy that I really don't think he did much wrong.

Many the time, though, I remember Charlie coming home from school and Stephen going, 'Well, go on then. Tell Mummy before I tell her!' And Charlie would sheepishly hold his hands out and show me that he had red marks across them from where he had been caned, and tell me the latest story of what he definitely hadn't done. And I'd put cream on his hands to soothe them and tell him, 'Now, behave yourself. Don't do that no more.'

I wasn't against caning if it was done properly, like just a bit of a tap when a boy had really misbehaved. But sometimes I thought the teachers really took it too far. I remember the boys had a friend called Wayne, a really tall ginger lad. And his mum always used to send him to school in short trousers, while I would send mine in long trousers. One day they came home and asked if Wayne could borrow a pair of theirs, although they wouldn't tell me why at first. But then I found out he had been caned across the back of his legs, down low where everyone could see. And I thought that was too hard, that was beyond discipline, and really horrible for the poor boy.

One thing that made me laugh about Little Charlie though, was how smart he was at picking things up that he heard me saying, without me even realizing. I remember one parent's evening at South Park Primary School, which was when I learnt that I really had to watch what I said in front of him.

I arrived and walked over to Charlie's teacher, but as soon as she saw me she started laughing. 'What's wrong?' I asked, all worried.

'Let's have a quiet word,' she said. 'I've been meaning to tell you this for a good while. But Charlie picks up a lot of what you say when you are obviously joking, and then repeats it as fact.'

'What do you mean?' I asked, confused – and a bit worried at what on earth he had been saying to her.

'Well, first of all, according to Charlie, you are only twenty-one and a half and, don't take this the wrong way, but I know you are well over that age.'

And true enough, that is something I always said whenever the kids used to go, 'How old are you Mum?' It was just a throwaway reply to avoid answering, and it made me chuckle that that's what he'd been telling people. Good to know he didn't question that I looked older, and I was more than happy for him to repeat that!

'And the second thing, I hope you don't mind me telling you, but I have to laugh about it.'

'OK . . .' I was concerned now, as she was going red!

'Well,' she said, 'he tells people you go down Piccadilly to earn a couple of bob.'

Oh, now it was my turn to go bright red. I didn't know where to look! Because you see this was something that my parents always used to say, that was a play on ladies of the night but didn't really mean that to anyone. It was just a throwaway reply you gave someone who asked where you were going when you didn't feel like answering. But Charlie had obviously taken notice of it and repeated it!

'My parents had a saying . . .' I stuttered.

But the teacher continued, 'Don't worry, mine always said things like that too. Obviously I don't think you do that. As you can see, I am laughing, so I took it as a joke. I hope you don't mind, but I told the other teachers as we all know it's not true. It just gave us a good laugh!' And, honest to God, she just stood there and roared while I wanted to sink into the ground. All I can say, is I was bleedin' glad they realized it was a joke! Can you imagine? 'School Cook Moonlights as Lady of The Night' . . .

At the same time as I was working at the school, I also had another job. As I said, Charlie had got it into his head that he wanted to own a shop of some sort for his next job, and had been hunting around to find one, and eventually he went out and bought himself a green-grocer's. I can't remember the name of it, but it was in a little side road over in Stratford. It took no time at all to get there from Barking as there was a main road that just drove straight between them.

The shop sold fruit and vegetables and eggs, and Charlie worked there full time, seven days a week. It was hard work, but he enjoyed it well enough – Charlie liked any job where he got to deal with people, and where talking and knowing everyone was a key part of the job!

And whenever I had any spare time around the school dinner work, I would hop on a bus and go down and work in there as well. So there you go – after aiming to have no jobs, I now had two! But I did it, and there was no option other than to do it, as Charlie didn't really want to have to fork out for another member of staff. Then again, look where it has got me today – I was six foot tall, but now I've got a hump on my back and am down to four foot, ha!

After a while me and June would go over to Stratford on the bus really early on a Saturday morning and we'd get her to help out too. She wasn't happy about it, though! June was just finishing off with school and had begun to go out on a Friday night with friends. She had also started drinking, which we weren't happy about as she was still young, but she was a hard one to control. She was a real rebellious teenager was June, and I think she would say the same now. Oh, we did struggle to control her at times. June did what June wanted to do at that age and we were in a constant battle with her as she tried to prove her independence.

I remember one particular weekend when we were on the bus on the way to the greengrocer's – it was one of those old-fashioned buses with the open platform at the back – and she started complaining that she didn't feel well and was going to be sick. I knew straight away that she was hungover, and I was furious! 'Don't you dare or I'll kill ya,' I said to her. But she went and stood on the back platform to get some air. Then the next minute she was sick as the bus was going along, and it hit the car behind. I was so embarrassed and angry with her! I really told her off that day.

Other Saturdays all the kids would come down, and we'd get everyone bacon butties and sit out the back of the shop having a catch-up. We'd sometimes get the younger kids to help out, but more often than not they would spend their time just eating the fruit, especially Charlie!

Well, after a year or eighteen months of running the greengrocer's, we had an inspection by the council. And it turned out we were in trouble with them for two reasons we didn't even know about.

In those days they were awful strict about who could sell eggs, and unbeknown to us, we weren't allowed to. Well, my husband tried to tell them that the people who had owned the shop before us had sold eggs, and so it was just something that we had continued. In fact, they had also sold chicken, but that was something we had decided against. But the inspector said he wasn't interested in the past tenants and, besides, that wasn't all that was wrong – he had a second problem with our shop.

He said the stuff we were selling was sticking out into the pavement too much 'cause we had crates and things on show for people to choose from out front. Apparently we had exceeded our space allowance, so we ended up with a fine.

It felt really unfair as it really wasn't something we were aware of. We were just new to the whole shop-owning thing. And although I forget the amount, we were given what at the time seemed like a very large bill – definitely disproportionate to our so-called crimes. It just kind of left a bad taste in our mouths, so Charlie went, 'Sod it, I don't want this shop no more. I'm selling it.' So he did. And although someone bought it, I heard that it closed down soon after. Not that it would be standing now even if it had survived the years, though – by my reckoning it is bang in the middle of the Olympic site! So yes, that would have spelt the end of it.

But getting rid of the greengrocer's did not mean the end of Charlie's desire to own a shop – he just went and bought a newsagent's instead! I'd hoped by selling the first shop I'd have been freed up in my hours a bit – I was finding it a struggle doing two jobs again. But no, I was in the new shop as often as the old.

Again, I can't remember the name of the place – if it even had one – but I remember it was in Bennetts Castle Lane in Dagenham. It was a tiny little narrow shop that sold sweets, tobacco and newspapers, and that was pretty much it.

Straight away I realized us taking on that shop was not a good idea. The biggest problem was the news-papers as Charlie had to get up at 4 a.m. to get them in. That was a killer!

But the sweet shop bit of it suited me, and I was more than happy to serve in there. You would weigh out the sweets from these big jars into these scales and put them in paper bags. We would sell them in quarters, and one quarter cost about a shilling, if that. It wasn't much at all. And while I served other people, I would serve myself at the same time! I probably ate more than I sold, much to Charlie's disgust. I never really had a favourite – I liked anything and everything, and would just dig into them all. But Charlie would create such a fuss, 'You know they've got to be paid for!' and all that. Blah, blah, blah. But I couldn't resist. I loved all the jars and the sugary smell. It made me think of the old days when my mum used to smuggle sweets home from the factory where she worked, and save them in a side drawer for treats.

Yep, my sweet tooth was as strong as ever, so this shop was great for me – and bad as well, if you know what I mean. You wonder why I have had to get a brand new set of teeth since!

The most popular, if I remember, were sherbet pips, which were these little tiny things, like hard balls or pips, in different fruit flavours on the outside, with bits of sherbet in the middle. Then there were rhubarb and custards, and Army & Navy sweets, which were black hard-boiled sweets that had a kind of liquorice flavour. They tasted like cough sweets. They're hard to get hold of these days. Even when you find 'em in those old-fashioned sweet shops that are all the trend now, well, the sweets just ain't the same.

So I went down most Saturdays, while the kids were left at home to look after themselves, and June would help out quite a lot in that shop too, both at weekends and then in the evenings. By then she had left school and was spending her days working in a hairdresser's. She had always been interested in doing hair. Back when we were in the pub she had done a bit of work as a Saturday girl in a hairdresser's down Roman Road which was nearby. When we moved to Ilford she had tried to keep it up, but it was too far to travel, so she had let the idea of hairdressing slide, until she left school at fifteen and then took on a job as a junior. As it was daytimes, though, she was able to help us out in the shop at other times.

The two younger girls used to love coming to the shop too. Susan and Carol would come along with me and play at running a sweet shop as they were so fascinated by it all. They could spend hours lining up all the sweets and pretending to serve customers.

One exciting thing about running the shop was that we had a famous customer who would come in there – Dudley Moore. The actor was especially famous at the time for his partnership on various BBC shows with Peter Cook. Peter was the tall fella and Dudley was the little 'un. His mum lived just down the road from the shop so I guess that is why he would pop in whenever he was around.

I never met him when he came in as I always seemed to be in and out all the time on errands and going to and from my dinner lady duties, but Juney used to tell me when he had been in. It was a good little claim to fame for our shop anyway.

But after a couple of years, running the shop became too much. Both me and Charlie were permanently exhausted from it, and again it was taking me away from the kids more than I liked. It wasn't making enough money for it to be worth our while, so we decided to get rid of it. I recently went by and saw that it is still there, but as far as I'm concerned, it doesn't look as nice as when we had it.

Owning your own shop is a tough business. It takes a lot of hours and commitment, and as with any business you own yourself, if anything goes wrong, you are the ones who take the direct hit. That was one of the reasons we had moved out of the pub, but at the time Charlie still hadn't been ready to take his orders from someone else. It was only after he'd tried running the two shops, and found both of them felt like harder work than they were worth, Charlie got frustrated and eventually went back to the normal way – working for other people!

LEFT: Here I'm behind the bar of the Rising Sun with my daughter June, who started helping us out for a few hours when she was twelve – though if asked, I'd swear blind she was eighteen.

BELOW: With the Rising Sun's women's darts team! We were terrible to start with, but eventually we managed to win some tournaments.

BELOW: Dad (*middle row, second in on the right*) and Uncle Joe (*middle row, second in on the left*) outside the Rising Sun, about to head off on a beano, a few years before Charlie and I took it over.

LEFT: Dad with Bet, who he courted for twenty years before he finally tied the knot. He asked for my approval before he got married.

RIGHT: My daughter Susan, aged fourteen.

LEFT: My daughter Carol down Petticoat Lane market in 1975. People would pay to have their photo taken with a monkey.

RIGHT: For years our holidays were spent at our caravan in Leysdown on the Isle of Sheppey. I loved it there, though it was harder to get away when we were running the pub. Here I'm with (*from left*) Uncle Joe, Aunt Mary, my June and Mary's daughter Linda.

ABOVE: Then in the mid-seventies we actually went abroad to Benidorm. This is a photo of a bullfight we went to see and that's my Charlie in the bullring. Trust him to put his hand up when they asked for volunteers! Luckily it was only a young bull, so not really dangerous.

LEFT: Riding a donkey was probably the most dangerous thing I ever did on holiday.

LEFT: Essex here we come! I reckon this must have been the Queen's Silver Jubilee, with Charlie decorating our house, and himself, in the Union Jack.

BELOW: Here we are all dressed up for a family wedding. I'm responsible for doing all the perms! From left to right, standing, are June, Susan, me, Little Charlie, Big Charlie and behind us are Aunt Mary's daughter-in-law Irene and her son Jimmy. At the front are Carol, my granddaughter Kelly and Carol's boyfriend at the time, David.

RIGHT: Charlie was especially fond of fancy-dress parties. Here he's sat with June.

ABOVE: My two Charlies.

RIGHT: Carol with her proud dad on her wedding day. She was about to marry a fella called Mark Wright.

RIGHT: The kids all together. From left to right: Susan, Stephen, Charlie, June and Carol.

TOP RIGHT: With Charlie on holiday in Cyprus – you can tell Charlie's been in the sun!

BOTTOM RIGHT: And here's a much more formal photo – one for the album. I'm wearing the outfit I'd bought for Little Charlie's wedding a few weeks before and Charlie looks very dapper in his suit. We were married for fifty-two years and Charlie always made me feel loved and protected.

ABOVE: Charlie surrounded by his grandkids. He doted on them all.

RIGHT: Here are three of the grandchildren, my Carol's kids: Joshua, Mark and Jessica.

ABOVE: It hardly felt real when *TOWIE* won a BAFTA in 2011. I was completely embarrassed by all the attention. Here I am with the cast of *TOWIE*. Standing on the left are Kirk Norcross and Joey Essex, with two producers from the show. There's me holding the award, then Sam Faiers, Lydia Bright, Amy Childs and Lauren Goodger. Arg (*left*) and my grandson Mark (*right*) are at the front.

TOWIE has meant I'm invited to all sorts of glamorous events. Here I'm with Carol, Natalya, Jessica and Mark at the launch of Jessica's Lipstick Boutique collection.

ELEVEN

The Life and Soul of the Party

Now, just because he had given up the pub didn't mean Charlie was going to give up the socializing! Oh no, far from it. And, in fact, not only did he want to socialize, but I suppose there was a bit of him that wanted to be sure he was always at the centre of any of the socializing as well. He had loved the social aspect of the pub – it was just the heavy lifting, maths and paperwork that he wanted to stop.

So the portable bar we brought with us from The Rising Sun was in the lounge of our new house. And once the neighbours had warmed to the idea of us being in their street after all, we were able to invite some of them round for drinks. Charlie would be in his element, standing behind the bar serving them, chatting away and holding court. Before we knew it, we were at the centre of the social scene in Ilford, and not just on our street.

He started going to the working men's club in Barking, and soon after joined the committee and ended up as Vice Chairman. He would go there every evening at the weekend, as well as one night in the week, and once we no longer had either of the shops, he would go at lunchtime at the weekend as well.

And, well, let's just say, you always knew when he was on his way home! He liked to have a good singsong did Charlie after a few drinks, and it didn't matter whether he was on his own. We could always hear him coming along the road – and so could the neighbours. They used to say they loved hearing him sing as it happened, rain, sunshine or snow, and they'd joke that they would hear him going over the same song lines again and again and think, 'I wish he'd hurry up and finish that song and move on to the next!'

'When Your Old Wedding Ring Was New' was his favourite choice of song, and he'd draw out every line for maximum effect as he sang it the whole way through. Honest to God, he used to drive us mad with that song.

Then in later years when the series *Neighbours* first started on television, he obviously thought that was a funny song to sing as he turned into our road. I'd hear him coming, willing him to hurry up, and when he got near the house I'd pull him in, hissing, 'Get in here and stop singing, for Christ's sake!'

Other times he drove to the club and back, which I wasn't happy about, as he would still have a good few drinks, but there was no stopping him.

Except for the nights I went along too, that is. On a Saturday night I would join him, and we'd go to the club together. I would drink lager and lime while he got rightly stuck into the pints of bitter, rounded off at the end of the night with the last couple being a 'little drop of whisky'. Well, it was him who claimed they were 'little' . . . not me; I'd say they were generally doubles! And we'd be sat around a table talking with half a dozen or more men and women who we had made friends with in the club, just having a chat about what had been happening that week or what have you. And then at some point someone would be sure to start singing a song and everyone else would join in. Or one of the old boys would get up and start telling stories or jokes. When I describe it now it sounds boring, and in some way I didn't enjoy it that much as it wasn't really my thing. Despite the years in the pub, I still wasn't really a drinker, so I tended to get tired of the evening before Charlie. But there were times we had a real laugh and a joke, and it hardly cost us anything. The price of alcohol in the working men's club was cheaper than in a normal pub, so being the seventies, you could still get drunk on a fiver.

But I would always be ready to leave before my husband and be like, 'Hurry up, let's go' all the time to Charlie. And when I finally got him to leave, we'd walk and catch the bus, which would stop at nearby South Park, and I always hoped the air on the way home would sober him up. Or other times, if he was too drunk and couldn't really walk, we would have to get a cab home. There was no driving our car when I was there too, though – I wouldn't allow that!

The kids were old enough that I was happy leaving them at home alone on those evenings – and, to be honest, they were well enough used to it, having looked after themselves all the time in the pub. They'd always laugh and say they could hear us coming home, 'cause of course there would be him trying to sing and me trying to stop him.

'Come on, Charl', let's get in.'

'When your old—'

'Shh, for goodness' sake!'

'Wedding ring—'

'Charlie!' I would hiss.

'Was new . . .'

And the kids would look out the window and see him swaying his way up the path. I'd go in first to try and stop the kids seeing their dad in such a state. 'Come on, kids!' I'd say, trying to get them on up to bed. But more often than not they would look out just long enough to see Charlie falling into next door's garden!

Our neighbours Mr and Mrs Watts had a privet hedge dividing their property from ours, and it had something else in with it that had prickles in it and Charlie was forever falling in it and getting the thorns in him. Then he'd be up and swearing, before stumbling on into the house. Not that it stopped him doing it again.

As for the kids, left alone in the house for the evening, I am sure I only found out afterwards some of the ways they found to entertain themselves . . .

As a fivesome they were very, very close, which was great. And they'd sit up together at night, chatting and listening to records – they would raid our collection apparently, and Stephen would be in charge of looking after the music. So they ended up with Des O'Connor or Max Bygrave, which were our records, as that was about all they could find. Or when they started getting their own music, they were able to enjoy Elvis, The Beatles, The Monkees, and one song that June loved but Carol hated – 'Young, Gifted and Black' by Aretha Franklin. There were always rows, I'm told, when that one went on the record player!

Or they'd watch telly, although that shut down early them days and they didn't have a lot of choice. I think there were only three channels at the time – BBC1, BBC2 and ITV – and the latest they would be showing anything was midnight, before the ol' test card appeared on the screen for the night. If I remember, it was a girl playing noughts and crosses with a clown. Why that was the image there all night, I have no idea, but it was!

One way to entertain themselves that the kids came up with one night as they sat up together waiting for us to come back from the club makes me shiver to think of it – it was a Ouija board. They were all like, 'What shall we do?' and someone apparently suggested a Ouija board, as I guess it had been talked about at school, and they did it a couple of times – not that we found out till later!

It sounds like they scared themselves silly that evening. They made the board out of paper and used a glass from the kitchen as the indicator, and then they sat there for hours trying to invite in the spirits of dead people to give messages through the board.

Well, no one ever told me what it started to spell out, but whatever it was frightened the life out of them. No one has ever owned up to pushing the glass around, so who knows if it was really a ghost or whatever, or if one of them was winding the rest up. But anyway they told me they also heard a noise upstairs, and then the dog started barking, so that was it – they were literally sat there screaming! In the end they panicked so much they decided they had to burn the board to cancel out the bad they thought they had done, so they went into the yard and did just that. And, I tell ya, while they might have been in bed by the time we got home that evening, none of them slept one wink that night, that was for sure!

Another time we were unimpressed by the evening's entertainment was when we came home to find one of the windows had been smashed. It didn't take long to realize a football had been the cause, and despite Stephen and Charlie's best attempts of being in bed already and pretending to be asleep, and then denials of any knowledge, it was pretty obvious they were the culprits!

The children were slowly but surely expanding their own social circles, though. All the kids had made good friends with the local kids and were always off playing with them. A fair few of these friends were around our house of a night when we were out, I am sure, although they have always denied to me that they actually had any parties. But as long as the friends had been sent on their way before we were home and the place had been tidied, I didn't mind too much.

As for mine and Charlie's social life, between the club and having people over for drinks at least once a week, we had built up quite a set of friends in the area. But one pair of friends we were sorry to lose, about a year after moving in, was our copper friend across the road, and his wife.

He retired at that time, and they had decided to emigrate to Australia. They were so excited about it and talked about nothing else in the months leading up to it. It had been a dream of theirs for years, and then finally they sold their house and had a big leaving party. Well, I remember the morning we stood outside the house to wave them off. I felt really sad as I thought that was the last we would ever see of them. And, as I can't write very well, I wasn't going to keep in touch with them by letter, so I thought that was the end of it.

Well, just two weeks later, I got a knock at my door and I nearly had a fit when I opened it to see her standing there. She just broke down crying as soon as she saw me, and I was like, 'What are you doing back? Come in, come in!' I sat her on the sofa and got her a cup of tea, settling myself down for a long conversation. I thought to myself that she must have left her husband for some reason or another.

But then she went, 'We had to come home, I was so homesick. I hated it. We just couldn't settle.'

I nearly spat out my tea. 'But you've not been out there a week!' I went.

She was determined, though. 'We didn't like it. We know we want to live back here.'

But then she got upset all over again because she knew she couldn't have her old house back as there were new people just moved into it, so she just sat and cried her eyes out.

Well, I didn't know what to make of it all. They managed to find a place to live in the end, although they had to move a bit further out than Ilford. But it just proves that the East End and Essex run through your veins. Once they've got under your skin, nowhere else will ever live up to them!

TWELVE

Mischief and Mayhem

Our two boys were always together and kept themselves active non-stop – out exploring with other local boys, playing in the park, and befriending everyone they came across. They even managed to make friends with one very special neighbour – Frank Lampard Senior! Frank and his wife, Pat, lived ten doors down from us at number 7 Chudleigh Crescent, and at the time he was playing for West Ham. Of course, the boys thought he was the greatest. So can you imagine when a couple of times he took them over to Barking Park for a kick-about? Oh, they were very happy with that!

Another time Stephen did what was called 'bob-a-job' for him. He was in the Scouts, and each year they would raise money for charity by going round the neighbours, saying, 'bob-a-job, guv?', which was them basically offering to do a job for a bob – 5p. I remember that Frank got him to sweep the yard for him for that.

Then you would get other famous football players coming round to visit him as well, and although I forget most of their names, they always attracted a bit of a crowd of local kids, especially Bobby Moore. He would come round on a Saturday after training or a match, or whatever it was they would have been doing as they both played for West Ham at the time. Bobby would arrive in this great big Rolls Royce, a real fancy car, and the boys would call out to him, giving their comments on the latest game or whatever. June had her picture taken with him once, which she was very proud of. Frank's wife, Pat, was lovely too. She had a hairdresser's at Faircross in Barking and was a huge West Ham supporter.

A few years later when she gave birth to Frank Lampard Junior she used to let Susan take him out in the pram 'cause Susan loved kids. They were a nice family and lovely neighbours, although they never came to our house parties, I have to say! I was sorry when I heard years later that Pat had died of pneumonia.

Sadly, though, Frank wasn't able to keep Charlie occupied often enough, so he was forever off causing trouble and mischief by himself.

I always used to say if there was ever a puddle, Charlie would find it and jump in it. And even if it was the hottest day of the year, and no puddle should even have existed, he'd still manage to find one!

I remember one day when he was about ten and he went off over the park. It was a sunny day so I had my windows open, and I heard one of the neighbours shouting, 'Charlie, your mother will kill you if you go in the house in that state. Don't even think about going in!'

Well, I looked out the door, and there he was, covered head to foot in green slime. Turned out he had been swinging on a rope over the river, fallen in and got covered in all the slime lying on the surface of the water. And it stank!

'Don't you dare come in this house!' I yelled out the window.

'Yeah, but Mum, it wasn't—'

'I don't want to hear who done it! You done it, now wait there!'

And I went off and got a bucket of cold water and made him stand out the front of the house and take off every last bit of clothing, putting it into a black bin bag as it was all ruined. Then I chucked the water over his head. I was so angry, and he was really embarrassed, but I hoped it would teach him a lesson. Of course, it didn't, and he went and found a new puddle the very next day!

Then there was another time Little Charlie caused me no end of grief . . . can you see a theme here?!

I had decided to keep him home rather than letting him play out, just to try and keep him out of trouble for a day. But he started tormenting me and was getting in my way as I was trying to do jobs around the house.

'Go down the shed and tidy it up. Entertain yourself down there, please, Charlie,' I said. Big mistake.

A couple of hours of blissful peace later, I realized things were far too quiet and I looked out the window, only to see Charlie happily painting our fence green. Not only that, but worst of all, he had painted the dog green! Poor Rex, who would let Charlie do anything to him, had stood there patiently as Charlie had covered him in this vile green paint. I was so mad! I walloped him all around the garden for that one, part furious, part panicking what Big Charlie would have to say about it.

And sure enough, he was furious. We all took turns at trying to clean Rex, but the more we scrubbed at him, the more he cried about it. So we decided to leave him overnight. The next day I couldn't find Little Charlie or Rex, and with a sense things could be going even worse, I went down to the shed. There was Charlie with a razor, just finishing off shaving Rex, who had not a stitch of fur left on him, except for his ears. 'Look, Mum,' he said all proud of himself. 'I've got all the paint off!'

Oh, I can laugh now, but back then . . .

Meantime, there was plenty of trouble with Carol too. While Big Charlie had always been keen on the partying, he was less than happy when the kids got old enough to start doing the same. As I said earlier, June had started drinking and going out around the time she finished school. On the one hand, it seemed hard to stop her when she was actually working and holding down a job as that meant she was behaving like an adult in one way. But as far as Charlie was concerned, she was still a child – and while she was living under our roof, it was his decision what she could get up to.

He set her a curfew of 10 p.m., which sometimes she obeyed, and sometimes she didn't. When she stayed out later than that it would drive him crazy, and he'd be prowling around the house until she was home. Then you would hear her try and creep in, but he'd be standing at the top of the stairs waiting for her. 'What time do you call this?' he would bellow, always followed by a few choice words. As June was the eldest, he probably was strictest with her as he wanted her to set an example for the rest of the kids. But she was quite a rebellious teenager and mostly did as she pleased.

Susan, though, was very well behaved and never even really wanted to go out as she became a teenager. She was quite happy doing her own thing. Or when she did go out, there was no question she would be home before the curfew.

But the same can't be said of our Carol. She had been well behaved when we first moved to Ilford because she was all clingy and then became wrapped up in her gymnastics and that. But as she got older, she was a wild little thing at times and was incredibly naughty – she never took any notice of the curfew at all, just coming back at whatever time she pleased. Oh, even when she was just fourteen, I remember the nights she didn't come home at all, and Charlie would get so angry he would go out and find her.

There is one time that I remember better than any other. She had gone out with her friend Georgina to Tiffanys, a club just round the corner from us in Ilford High Road. There were always singers performing down there, and the two of them used to love getting up on stage with them. But Charlie had banned them from going there, saying Carol was too young to be in a place like that.

Now, every Friday night Charlie would go out for a few drinks – he had finished work for the week and liked to wind down with a few pints. This one particular Friday he got home and asked if all the kids were in yet. Well, I said that yes, they were, as I always did, even if they weren't. I'd swear blind they were in by then to protect them from their father, and I even sometimes stuffed their beds to make it look as though they were sleeping!

That night I had Carol's bed bunged with all sorts of things – clothes, a mop, even a wig where her head should be poking out! But this time he didn't fall for it. 'She's not in!' he said. 'Where is she? Down that bleedin' club of her's, Tiffanys, I bet!'

He'd taken his shirt off 'cause it was a hot night, and he had a vest on underneath. Not any old vest, though – he was wearing a string vest. Before I could protest, he called up to Little Charlie, 'Come on, get yourself ready. We're going to Tiffanys!'

Little Charlie was only about eleven at the time, but looked a good few years older. And he was about as tall then as he is now. Even at that time he could hold his own.

'Charlie! You can't—' I said, trying helplessly to stop him.

'Nope, I am not having my daughter in that club at this time. It's a disgrace and I told her she wasn't to go there. I'm not having her go against me, so I'm going to get her!'

I don't even think it was that late. It was more the principle that she had gone against him that made him so angry, I think.

166

Well, they went down there in the car and pulled up right outside in the front of the door. There was a big queue of people waiting to get in, and bouncers on the door, two big fellas, who were twice as big as my husband – and you know how big he was! Charlie marched straight up to the door and started to walk in, and they told him, as polite as could be, 'Sorry sir, you can't come in without a shirt and tie on.' A shirt and tie! And there was Charlie in his string vest! Well, Little Charlie was dying of embarrassment by this time as everyone was looking, so he had ducked right down in his seat, just peering over the bottom of the window to keep an eye. But there was no way these two big men were going to stop my husband – he was on a mission.

'I am looking for my daughter, Carol Brooker, who should not be in here. So get out of my way! Out of my way!' He yelled and pushed past them. Well, then they had to let him in, and poor Little Charlie was still sat outside cringing in the car. He has told me since, 'Mum, I'll never ever forget that image. Never in a million years!'

Meantime, there were Carol and Georgina, singing and dancing away inside the club, having the time of their lives. Until someone said to her, 'Haha! Carol, your dad is here – and he's only got a string vest on!'

Well, you can imagine. She was mortified. And the

two of them ran into the toilets as quick as could be, hiding before Charlie could spot them.

Then a manager came over to Charlie, who was marching around the club looking for Carol. Everyone was watching as the manager asked Charlie what was happening, and my husband told him, 'You know my daughter is only fourteen? She should not be in here.'

'Well, I'm sorry,' he said, 'but she told us she was sixteen. But now I know and I can assure you she will not be allowed in here again!'

So that was Carol ruined for any future visits to the club. Her real age had been given away and she'd been caught out good and proper.

I'm sure she didn't think she could feel any more embarrassed than she already did, but then the manager put an announcement out over the tannoy: 'Would Carol Brooker please make herself known as her father is here to collect her.'

Oh, she died. Well, she wouldn't come out of the toilets while Charlie was there, and sent a friend to tell the manager that. So Charlie done no more but come home and waited for her to come home after. But it turned out she had only come home to tell us her plans 'cause you had no mobiles or anything in them days.

'Right, that's it,' she said. 'I can't believe you embarrassed me like that. You don't realize how much you showed me up in front of all my friends and those boys. So I'm going! I'm leaving home now!' and she started packing her bags. She was crying her eyes out, and so was I, and I believed her and was pleading, 'Please don't go, Carol! Your dad didn't mean it. Stay here!'

Oh, I can laugh about it now, but it wasn't funny at the time.

And Carol just set her face into a scowl and left. She went round to Georgina's house for the night.

It was a cold night and Carol is like me – she can't stand the cold. But Georgina's family wouldn't put the heating on. So the next day she came back and said to me, 'Mum, they wouldn't put the heating on. Is it all right if I come back?'

Oh, I can tell you, I was so relieved. She told me Georgina's dad hadn't been very pleased about her coming round, and then added, 'He's just as bad as what Daddy is. So I want to come back, but you have to promise Dad won't moan at me any more.'

And that was it, she came back. But what a drama! Oh, there were some real tears as well as real laughter in that house!

THIRTEEN

Waste Not, Want Not

When we had been in Ilford for about four years, my work load at the school suddenly increased. After all my time as assistant cook, helping out the main lady, the head cook turned sixty and had to retire. There was no choice back then – sixty was retirement age and that was that.

So one day she said to me, 'How about you? Do you want to take over?'

Straight away I went, 'Nah,' but she was like, 'Go on. You'll get more money and you'll get to oversee this lot.'

I thought about it, and talked to Charlie, who thought it was a good idea as he knew I actually quite enjoyed it and the extra money was always useful. In school they had asked if anyone else was interested, but all the other women in the kitchen responded like, 'No, we do not want that bleedin' job!'

Eventually I said to them, 'Well, do you mind if I take it then?'

They held a meeting in the kitchen and everyone was asked what they thought about me taking over, and when they all said they were fine with it, I decided I would.

After that, I was paid a tenner a week, but the hours were longer. I was supposed to start at about 8 a.m., although I always went in earlier as I liked to give the place an extra clean and get the ovens on and heating, and generally get the place ready nice and early before the other ladies arrived.

Carol had convinced me to get a bike to speed up my journey time to and from the school each day, so I did. I got myself a simple bike that got me there and back each day. It was only about half a mile, but it was that bit quicker. The kids thought it was very funny to see me on it, but after a while I quite enjoyed it.

And I would be working at the school until 2.30 or 3 p.m., cooking for about 300 kids a day, as a lot of the time we had to make food for another school that didn't have a kitchen and send it out to them.

It was a bit lonely being the boss, though. All the people who had been my friends, despite them saying they didn't mind me being in charge, kind of turned against me once I actually became the boss. They changed the way they were with me. I used to say to them, 'I'm not going to moan at you or argue or anything. Just carry on the way you have always done things. However you want to do it, do it.'

And I wasn't bossy, I was nice, but they never were the same with me.

I remember telling Charlie about it, and he just said, 'Let them get on with it. You ain't there to be making friends. Besides, they'll sure as can be come running to you as soon as they want something.'

As part of being in charge I had to go to the town hall to do a course in cooking – all health and safety and the likes, as well as how to make the dishes exactly the way the council wanted them to be. I got through all that fine, but I used to get a bit frustrated that there wasn't no leeway on what we made the children each day. Once a week I was given a list of meals that the council had decided we should feed them. I suppose they put it all together from strict lists of what was good food, but probably, more than anything, what fitted into the budget. They were very specific about each meal and exactly how it had to be made. But, to be honest, I didn't think the menu had moved on much from when I was at school. There were a lot of the old classics, such as pies and potatoes and the likes.

But, of course, one of the favourites that appeared on that council list time after time was a bleedin' sausage plait! I'd never even heard of it back then and remember thinking, 'How the hell am I gonna make that?' I really and truly thought you had to put actual real sausages in it at first and then plait around them.

Well, you don't. What it is, is sausage meat, wrapped up in puff pastry, which is plaited over the top. It's actually pretty simple to make, doesn't cost a lot and looks impressive. I gradually learned that one, and once I knew how to do it, tell the truth, I quite enjoyed making it, and after that I did hundreds of them. I got so used to it, and did so many, I reckon at the finish I'd have been in the *Guinness Book of Records* for most sausage plaits ever made!

And I got so good and particular at them that I couldn't put up with anyone doing them wrong. I remember there used to be a young Indian girl there to help me out, but then she got a bit lazy about how they should be done. I used to go, 'No, that's not done properly. Look, it's all come undone! Do it again properly!'

I'm sure no one did them as well as me! In fact, if you want to know exactly how I make my perfect sausage plait, turn to page 299 for the recipe and give it a go yourself.

Kids are always funny about food, though. You'd

get some of them desperate for seconds – growing lads with big appetites, or skinny little things who looked like they weren't well fed at home and were desperate for their school lunch. And where I could, I would always slip them some extra.

Then there were those who never liked what was on offer, no matter what it was. 'I don't want that, Miss,' they'd complain to me. So I started a trick to get them to eat it. I'd have a load of sweets stashed in my pockets, and if a little 'un said that, I'd tell them, 'If you eat that, I'll give you a sweet afterwards.' And suddenly it would be, 'Oh, all right then!' and they'd grab their plate and head off with it.

I'm sure half of them used to go away and chuck their food in the bin when I wasn't looking, then come back with an empty plate and tell me they had eaten it all, just for a sweet. But ah well, I could only try!

After a while the food started to change a bit, to reflect the ethnic changes within the school. There were more Indian children joining, where it had been all white children in the beginning, and I had to go back to the town hall to learn some more dishes, this time curry and rice and the likes. That was all new to me, so it was interesting to learn something so different.

The council used to say that none of the food could be taken home, either while you were preparing it – 'cause of health and safety, I guess – or afterwards, because . . . Well, actually I never understood why.

And I'll be honest, I didn't follow either rule. Sometimes there was just too much preparation to do it all at work. Say, like in the lead-up to the school Christmas dinners I'd bring home a sack of potatoes and peel them indoors while I was sitting watching TV – it was the only way we could get everything done in time.

It used to annoy Charlie, but I would just tell him, 'That way I ain't got to bother doing it tomorrow,' and then I'd carry right on.

As for what was left over at the end of the day, we were told by the council that it had to be thrown away into bins, but it always seemed such a waste to me. It was perfectly good food – I should know! So if the girls asked if I minded them taking a tray or so of leftovers home, I'd just tell them to get it in their bag quick and head on.

And after a while I started doing the same myself. It seemed crazy to put all those helpings in the bin when I had made them. It was good food, and instead I had to go home and cook a new meal all over again for the family. So more often than not, dinner at my house was actually school lunch leftovers! It certainly made my evenings easier anyhow.

My kids would get home and ask, 'Mum, have you

got anything for me to eat?' and I'd point them towards whatever there was, say, a tray of that strawberry cake you used to get in school, a sponge cake with a jug of custard, or a tray of corned-beef pie.

I was glad, though, that I did that – starting to cook as soon as I had come home from a day of cooking would have been too much, even for someone like me who enjoys it!

Around this time it wasn't just my workload that had increased – Charlie was working harder than I'd ever seen him. Now that he was no longer running the shops, he was juggling several jobs and many a night would get just a few hours of sleep. He would leave the house early of a morning and come back late at night, as he was doing such crazy hours.

There was a bit of him that liked to be doing so many jobs, but I also think he didn't question it as he felt it was the man's role. He saw it that he was keeping his family in the best life he could, and that it was his job to do so. So he just got on with it.

Not that he did everything exactly by the book, of course. No, Charlie always made sure he could get a cheeky extra wherever he could! And why not? It was what everyone did and it was the kind of character my husband was. It was no different to my mum sneaking the sweets out of the factory in her turban as she had done years before, or me sneaking packets of sugar out of Tate & Lyle down my bra. You didn't abuse your position, but when times were hard it felt like you were entitled to a bit more. And, let's face it, bosses and company owners expected it.

Back in the East End, when Charlie and the mother-in-law had been working on the docks before we moved into the pub, it was quite easy to get that little extra something. There were crates constantly passing through the docks, and often enough one of them wouldn't be collected. The people working down there would be alerted to it, then they'd break it open and help themselves to a bit of what was inside. It could be toys, or food, or furniture, or beauty products . . . anything really.

So there were plenty of times back in Bray Drive, in Canning Town, when Charlie would come home with a bag full of goodies. They couldn't take that much at a time, though – there were always dock police on the lookout, so they had to be careful and just take a bag full. Besides, everyone was pretty decent about sharing it around, so one dock worker wouldn't clear out a container on his own.

Some of the stuff Charlie brought home we would keep, and some of it we would sell on to neighbours. I remember him coming back with a big black sack full of nail sets one Christmas Eve, for example. They were these little leather cases that had come from abroad, which had mini nail files and scissors in them. The girls were in their element – they loved them. Christmas Eve was perfect timing! Then the others we sold on to the neighbours, for half a crown or something like that.

We weren't the only ones at it – everyone survived by topping up their wages somehow. There just wasn't a lot of money about in the East End and your actual salary was rarely enough to live on, so people had to do what they did to survive, 'specially once they had a family. I guess that is why people always imagine East Enders to be all wheeler dealers, 'cause it was how we got by most of the time!

But once we were living out in Essex there was less of that kind of thing going on. People tended to be a little bit straighter and follow the rule book more. Not that it didn't happen still – it just wasn't quite as rife. Even Charlie was at it less, although if an opportunity presented itself, he wasn't the one who was going to say no.

I remember one time Charlie told me he had to go back into London to pick some things up. Well, him, Dad and our Stephen headed off in a van, down near where we used to live, I think, by Victoria Docks. And they came back with the van full of tins of something, salmon or corned beef, I think it was. Now, don't ask me where they got it from. Dodgy out of some crate down at the docks or something, no doubt. But the van was loaded high. And when they got home they swapped them all to this sort of outhouse kind of thing we had in the back garden, which was attached to the house, before covering them up with a blanket. I suppose Charlie put the word about a bit, and then all these people started coming round to buy the tins. No one ever asked where something was from if they were getting it on the cheap.

Oh, my husband always had his hand in something or other – or a bit of everything! But it was the East End way. It might have been a bit alien to Essex at that time, but since then I think that has changed. Gradually lots of big typical East End characters have moved to Essex. In a way, Essex is more like the old East End these days than the East End itself!

So one of the jobs Charlie had was delivering meat for a butcher's in Barking to local schools and what have you first thing in the morning, then he spent his day doing insurance and his night driving a cab.

Well, I could tell a few interesting stories about his morning deliveries. Say he was delivering chickens . . . if there was one left over at the end of his rounds, it would make its way to us rather than end up back at the butcher's. He'd bring it home at the end of his shift, and that would do for our dinner – if we weren't eating school dinners, that is! Yes, it was cheeky, but did anyone notice? No. And sometimes he took the boys along with him, so they saw how it worked.

So we had a freezer full of top-quality meat and chicken and we all got spoilt with the finest cuts. It got so ridiculous and we had so much extra meat that we even used to feed Rex on it. And do you know how used to it that dog got? When Charlie stopped the job and the freezer finally ran down to empty, we had to go back to normal meat. But not Rex, he wouldn't have it. The first time I put him down a dish of sausage meat after the freezer ran dry, he sniffed it, looked at me resentfully as though to say 'what the hell have you given me?' and turned tail and walked off! I couldn't believe it! He kept it up for the next few days as well, until he got so hungry, that with an angry bark he eventually wolfed it down. This was an Alsatian who was so used to the best steak the everyday stuff wasn't good enough. Crazy.

Not that Charlie's work always was a good thing for the dog. No, I remember this one night that we all felt so bad about – even today I feel guilty about it. Basically, Charlie would come home from work exhausted, and often not in the best mood. I could see why as he was really running himself down, but he wasn't always the easiest for us to deal with, and anything could set him off if he was in a foul mood.

Well, this one evening, one of the girls, I think it was Carol, was carrying a tray of drinks through from the lounge to the kitchen. There was a glass sliding door dividing them with a rail at the top and the bottom, but the door didn't fit exactly and hung out a bit.

Rex slept in the kitchen at the time and had a habit of putting his nose through the gap in the door and pushing it open when he wanted to get out, and he got pretty good at doing it.

This one evening Carol couldn't open the door as her hands were full, so she tried to push the door with her foot. Well, it only fell off the runner didn't it, and all the glass smashed on the floor. It made a terrible noise and there were bits of glass everywhere. Obviously there was no fixing this door.

Well, I panicked, didn't I, 'cause Charlie was due home soon and, bless him, I knew he'd go mad if he got in after a hard day's work to find a complete mess, something that had been caused by carelessness and that would be expensive to fix. I wanted to protect the kids, so I said, 'Right, all go to bed before Dad gets in. Quick, go!'

And I packed them all off to bed as quick as could be and started trying to tidy up. I was all nervous, and couldn't think what to say. So when Charlie came in I just said the first thing that came into my head, 'You'll never believe what happened. Rex was up to his old tricks opening the door, and it's fallen off the runners and smashed. But it's fine, we will get it fixed. It'll be all right.'

I thought that would be it and it wouldn't have mattered. I thought he would be angry but accept it, and I'd just have to put up with him having a bit of a rant and then maybe being in a mood for the rest of the evening.

Well, it clearly wasn't all right. For at that Charlie stormed off to kitchen, grabbed the dog by the scruff of the neck, and all we could all hear was him cursing the poor dog for the next while. Oh, I hated it. And I know the kids were so upset because they could all hear it as they lay up in their beds, listening to Rex getting punished for something he didn't do, while Carol got away with it.

I did feel bad about that. I know Charlie was just taking out his stress, and as far as he knew it was Rex's fault, but it wasn't fair on the dog at all. I made sure he got extra big pieces of steak for the next few days after that!

Not, of course, that we didn't get a few laughs out

of Charlie over his work too – it wasn't all stress and bother. There was one night I will never forget.

He was working on insurance for The Co-op, I think it was, The Co-operative Insurance. And he would be going around door-to-door to collect premiums off the customers, which was the money they would pay to be insured. Then he would also try and get new customers as well. I don't remember the exact details but it worked something like that.

One Friday evening me and the kids were all sat on the settee in the front room, just relaxing, watching TV and what have you, while we waited for him to come home from his day at work. Then June gave me a call from her work – by then she was working part-time as a barmaid in a pub called the Fly House in Faircross.

She could hardly speak for laughing, but said, 'Mum, I'm not gonna tell you what he's done, but keep an eye out for Dad coming home. He just called in here on his way back after work and, oh my life, he looks ridiculous.'

Well, we heard the front door open, and I was like, 'Behave, here comes your father. Behave!' And they all sat up, and Little Charlie, being nosey, put his head round the corner to see his dad.

'Oh,' he said. 'Mum, it ain't Daddy.'

'What do you mean, it ain't Daddy? It's got to be!' I said, confused. Then I shouted, 'Charlie, is that you? What's the matter?'

'Wait a minute! I'll be in in a minute,' he called back, sounding a bit odd.

Well, when he finally walked in, can you believe, he'd only gone and had a perm! You've never seen anything like it in all your life. He had let one of his customers' daughters do it because she was practising to be a hairdresser.

We were in hysterics. He had these awful, ridiculous tight curls. And June, well, apparently as soon as he had walked in the pub she had said, 'Dad, you look like a plonker. What have you done?'

But did he care? No, he thought he looked the bee's knees! But oh, it was terrible. I don't think the kids had laughed so much in their lives. Until the next week that is. He visited the same customer, came home again, and we had the same sort of game. Except this time when he came in the room, we were shocked to see that this girl had dyed his hair completely black. And I mean JET black. He had a moustache at the time and she had even dyed that! His hair and moustache had been going grey, but now they were as dark as anything. And he thought he looked wonderful, but it was terrible. I'll never forget it.

Oh, we had tears rolling down our cheeks. 'Whatever is wrong with you, you stupid man?' I asked him. But he just shrugged it off, and I had to put it down to another of Charlie's mad moments – life was never dull with him! And while I felt embarrassed to leave the house with him, he was more than happy to strut about and show off what he thought was his great new look.

Charlie came home with some tricks in his time, he did. But his attitude was that if it got him another customer, or kept one happy, that kind of thing was worth it. And as far as he was concerned, he had got himself a free hairdo in the process!

Then there was his cab driving of an evening. I don't remember too much about it because he would often get home late and tired and not be in the mood for talking, and I'd be worn out by that time too after doing my dinner lady job, seeing to the kids, doing all the washing, tidying, ironing and everything else. So late-night conversation and story exchanging wasn't really something we went in for.

But I do know he was doing private cabbing, so it was just in our family car, not in a black cab. And he worked for a company in Central London who would get him to go to all sorts of places in town. I'm sure he enjoyed it enough – again, being social is all part of a cabbie's job, so he no doubt talked the back legs off a lot of his customers!

So one thing that could never be said about my husband was that he was shy of work, and his mentality about working certainly rubbed off on the kids. June had always worked hard from a young age, with us in the pub, then at her hairdressing, and later on with her bar work.

And then when Susan was thirteen or fourteen she got herself a weekend job in a local pie and mash shop. She would help out serving the customers, and then'd bring us home some of it after she finished her shift on a Saturday night, which was always a nice treat.

Carol's first job was in a greengrocer's – not ours, but one in Faircross – while Stephen got his first job as a pot man – washing the dishes – in one of the local pubs when he was fourteen, before he started working in them as a DJ.

And Charlie, when he started doing his first Saturday job around fifteen, was working at a car mechanic's garage.

Them days it was easy enough to get a Saturday job, whereas today it is not so easy. Back then there was a lot on the go.

I used to tell my lot, if they wanted things, they had to help me out and pay for half of them as I couldn't afford it otherwise. I wanted them to learn to work and contribute, not just to expect that I would buy them anything they needed as they got older. And I think it worked. Yeah, they all copied their dad's grafting way of life, which still makes me feel proud of 'em now.

FOURTEEN

House of Fun

Back at the house, Charlie had decided our old portable bar was not good enough. He got it into his head that he wanted to build a proper private bar in our home! Oh yes, I kid you not. He wanted it to be properly kitted out with all the drinks, and to look almost like we had a bit of a pub in our living room.

So once he had decided, he went for it. We knocked through the lounge and the dining room to create one big room, then we had a fella come and put a bar in. It was a proper bar too, with a wooden top, and we stocked it with spirits and had the optics along the wall behind it and everything. There were shelves where the glasses were all stacked and a mirror over the top of the bar. We even had pumps on the bar, although they were for decoration really, and the beers were kept underneath the bar.

Even I, who was just imagining the trouble this new addition was going to bring, had to admit it was impressive. And everyone else thought the same. People used to come in and go, 'Cor, blimey! Ain't that good!' and you could see Charlie swell up with pride.

At the same time as we had that work done, we also had a huge great extension built so I could have a big kitchen with more space to cook. The old kitchen had been a tiny little cupboard, and had been the one real thing I hadn't liked about the house when we bought it.

Well, with all those changes taking place, it was inevitable that we'd end up spending even more time socializing when we invited people over to make the most of our new upgraded house. At first we just used to have a few friends over for a drink, but then it kept growing in size and, before you knew it, we were hosting all sorts of parties – sometimes for a reason, and sometimes just for the hell of it.

People would bring a bottle or two with them to add to our stock behind the bar, and I always did some catering and supplied a bit of buffet-type food for everyone.

Charlie was especially fond of fancy-dress parties as he liked dressing up and getting into a different role. There was a bit of him that could have made a great actor. He liked singing too, and having everyone's eyes on him, so a fancy-dress party was a good excuse for that.

It became 'specially popular to have a party around our house every New Year's Eve, and it was always fancy dress. I have some great photos from then with us and the kids all dressed up.

I remember one time Little Charlie dressed up as a black baby. We had painted him up and put a white napkin on him, although it didn't turn out that well so he ended up looking more like an Indian baby, a little Pocahontas kind of child! It doesn't seem right looking back, but at the time it would never have been thought of as inappropriate. As for Little Charlie, he was always the one we got to do the daftest things, but he was always so good natured and up for a laugh that he'd go along with pretty much anything.

As for me, there was no getting out of it either – I had to dress up too! I remember one year – I think it was the same year as Little Charlie's black baby outfit actually – when I was dressed as a clown. My husband had hired two clown suits, one for me and one for him, and we looked really funny. Being a large man, his looked huge, but he took it all very seriously!

Those were good parties, though. If you asked anyone local at that time what they were doing for New Year, they would have told you, 'Going over Charlie's, of course!' It was always 'Charlie's' rather than 'Charlie and Pat's', but I didn't mind that. I knew Charlie was the sociable one that everyone was friends with and I was the one in the background. But I was happy with that – it's where I felt more comfortable.

And one thing's for sure, Big Charlie needed no excuse to have a party. It didn't matter to him if it was Christmas, New Year, a birthday, or just any ol' day of the week. I remember one day when he said to me, 'We're having a party tonight.' And I was like, 'What? Charlie, you've given me no warning! I'm really not in the mood. Can't we do it another day? Why does it need to be tonight?'

No word of a lie, he looked around the room, looking for inspiration and shaking his head. 'No,' he said finally with a big grin on his face. 'It has to be today 'cause it's the canary's birthday.'

I tell you, I had no idea whether to laugh, cry or hit him!

As for the kids, we generally let them join in the parties. It seemed silly to send them up to their rooms while we partied below, so we would let them join us, and they were all great and could socialize well – a skill they had learned in their early years in the pub.

And as the kids one by one got nearer to drinking age, we tried to encourage them to start using the bar at home with their friends – we decided that having them drinking under our roof was safer than drinking who knows where. Yes, they might have been under age, but they were going to drink anyway, so at least that way we could keep an eye on them.

The girls were also starting to get boyfriends in their mid-teens, and Charlie was desperate to try and stop that, which I always thought was ironic given the hard time me and him had got off my dad. But he could never see that. As far as he was concerned it was different when it was his daughters, and he was going to do every-thing in his power to keep them innocent for as long as possible! So when they started courting, and say a boy came round to visit one of the girls and went up to their bedroom, Charlie would say, 'Where is he going?'

'Upstairs to see one of the girls,' I'd reply.

'No, he is not.' And he'd shout upstairs, 'You two! Get down here where I can keep an eye on you!'

And keep an eye on them he did . . . If we were sat in another part of the lounge, he was so blatant in the way he would twist and turn in his chair to watch what they were up to.

I'd say to him, quietly as I could, 'Stop it, Charlie. Don't. They're only sitting there talking.'

But he'd just say, 'I don't care. I'm not having none of that!'

As for the whole birds and the bees chat, I have to admit I wasn't very good at doing that with the girls. I suppose because I hadn't had that chat with my own mum – I was too young while she was alive, and then she had died by the time I needed it – I wasn't sure how to do it. It had been the older sister of a friend who had filled me in on the ways of the world, and I wasn't sure how to pass it on to my own children. But I still tried because I didn't want them to go through what I had.

So I did tell them about periods. I can't say I wasn't a bit embarrassed about it, but I did it, and they got it.

But when it came to the whole sex talk thing . . . I obviously left it too late! I remember I tried to tell June, and she went, 'Yeah, all right, I know what you're talking about. You don't need to tell me,' 'cause she had learned it all already – from this one and that one at school, I suppose.

Then later I psyched myself up to talk to another of the girls and she went, 'I already know, don't I. I know what it's all about!'

So in the end I just settled for saying, 'All right then, as long as you behave yourself, and know this, that and the other, that's fine. We are all in this together, so anything you need to know, you ask me or your sisters.'

It was a very different set of rules when it came to the boys' love lives, though, as far as Charlie was concerned, I tell ya. As Stephen and Little Charlie got older and began courting, my husband's attitude was to give them condoms and just say, 'Don't do anything wrong, and I don't want anything coming back.'

'Dad!' they'd go. 'We don't want them sort of things happening either! We're fine!'

'Nope! I want to be sure. Don't you dare let anyone knock on this door and say that they have your child. That is what I want to be sure of.'

Oh, it was a real difference for the boys and the girls – and June couldn't take being told what to do any more. By the time she was eighteen, she was desperate to prove her independence – but the way she went about it didn't go down well.

She had a boyfriend at the time called Donald, and straight away Charlie told her he wasn't right for her. But he said that about most of the lads the girls met, so she didn't take no notice – he never thought any of them were good enough for his daughters, like most dads, I guess. But really this time I had to agree with him.

And she came home one day and announced that she was pregnant and they were going to get married. Well, needless to say, I wasn't happy, but Charlie was downright furious.

And I'm not being funny but, as her mum, I knew she wasn't pregnant, despite her swearing blind that she was. You just know as a mum. So I went mad, and said, 'Why am I working and saving up all this money to get you married, as you haven't got any money of your own saved up for it, and you aren't even pregnant. What are you doing?!'

But she just set her mouth and told me, 'I want to get married. I have to get married.'

We were beside ourselves, but eventually we just had to go through with it. But even on the wedding day, Charlie was trying to change her mind. He went into her bedroom as she was having photos done, and said to her, 'You don't have to do this. I'm telling you now, please don't go through with it.'

It was not in Charlie's nature to beg, so you can see how desperate he was to stop it.

But she insisted he was fine and went through with it anyway. She was a stubborn young lady was June.

So she moved out and in with her husband down the road, and soon after she really fell pregnant. And I remember that when she was pregnant I got a bit of a shock when I thought I was pregnant as well. I was horrified as I really didn't want another child. Don't get me wrong, I absolutely love all five of my children, but there was no way I wanted a sixth. I had told Charlie after we had Little Charlie that there was no way he was getting more out of me, and I stuck to it.

By then I was thirty-nine and my youngest child, Little Charlie, was twelve. I know a lot of people don't become mums until they are thirty-nine these days, but it was not for me. I was not up for taking on another baby. But my periods had stopped so it was all I could think it could be. So with a heavy heart I went to the doctor's with June, and said, 'Please can I do a test – but don't tell me I'm pregnant!'

And he was all for joking about it, and said, 'That's handy! You two can go through the delights of pregnancy together!'

Well, I wasn't amused. 'Tell me I'm pregnant,' I said, 'And I'll commit suicide! I can tell you now, if I am, I don't want it, and you need to give me something to get rid of it.'

Well, as it turned out, my change was coming on – I hadn't seen it coming at all and had no warning signs, but I was finished with the time of the month, for life. Thank God!

But I couldn't wait for June to give birth, and was excited about meeting my first grandchild. When she went into labour I went down to the hospital to wait, although I wasn't allowed in the room with her. So I sat out in the corridor all excited with Charlie, until I was allowed to go in to see her and her new baby girl, who she decided to call Kelly. And this little girl had popped out with a beautiful head of ginger hair and was so lovely! Charlie was over the moon too. He loved her instantly and doted on her from the moment he set eyes on her.

We always looked after Kelly and spoiled her – I guess you do with the first one. Charlie put aside his differences with June's husband and we spent as much time with Kelly as we could. It is a grandparent's right to just spoil the kids, knowing you don't have to be strict as you were with your own kids. At the end of the visit you just open the door and say, 'Ta ta,' as they head back to their parents, who have to deal with that side of things!

So while June was getting to grips with being a mum, it was funny watching the other two girls with their boyfriends. They were a lot more confident that I had been with my Charlie when I had first met him as a shy seventeen-year-old girl and he had come round from the local council to do some work on our house. I couldn't even speak at first, despite his cheeky banter! And it took a little while before we began courting. But not with my lot. They were much more confident.

I remember Susan having her first boyfriend when she was around sixteen, but it was the way Carol used to behave that I always found myself shaking my head at. Carol went out with this lad, I forget his name, and he would call round, all devoted like. But if she didn't feel like going out with him, she had this trick she used to pull.

She would go upstairs and get herself all dressed up and ready for the night, then put a dressing gown on over her clothes and come back down again. 'Oh, I'm sorry, I can't come out tonight. I don't feel well so I think I am just going to go to bed.'

'OK, Carol,' he'd say. 'I'll just go home then. Hope you feel better soon.'

Well, the first couple of times she pulled that one, I didn't realize what was going on, and I'd say to him, 'Oh, don't worry, you don't have to go home. Just stay around for the evening if you want and watch TV.'

Then I'd see she would be scowling at me and gesturing wildly for me to let him go. So off he would head, and no sooner had he got out the door and climbed into his car than the dressing gown was off and Carol would be heading out the door for an evening of fun with her friends. I always used to say to her, 'You wait till you get married and your kids behave like that . . .' but she would just shrug it off.

I was determined the other girls were not going to make a mistake and get pregnant before they were married, as was becoming more and more common amongst people their age, so I tried to suggest to them that they go on the contraceptive pill – although obviously I said it without Charlie knowing. There was no way on earth he would agree with me about it, but I had to do what I thought was best for them. I remember I said to them, 'Keep this between me and you because, for God's sake, if your father finds out, he will have an absolute canary fit. He'll go completely mad.' But I think they were sensible girls really, despite my worries.

One of my favourite memories from around this time, as the girls were gaining their freedom, was them learning to drive. The best bit about that was that Rex started to learn the sound of their car engines, so he would be there waiting when they got home. He would often lie at the top of the stairs and keep an eye on everything in the house. He'd take no notice of any passing car – until he heard the sound of one of the girl's cars, then he would be down the stairs like a shot, waiting for them to walk in.

But while the girls' attention was now firmly on boys, Stephen and Charlie were wrapped up in boxing.

Their love of the sport that Charlie had instilled in them with the ring back in the pub continued, and once they were teens they took up boxing at Barking Boxing Club. Most kids were put through non-competitive training first, but as my two already knew what they were doing, they were put into competitive boxing straight away. They fought all over the place – Southend, Romford, the East End – and they did all their training together. They were always together really.

I think as a sport, though, it was probably more in Little Charlie's nature than in Stephen's. Even when they were smaller, and despite Charlie being the younger brother and quite little for his age, he would always stick up for Stephen. So if he saw someone giving Stephen a bit of hassle in the playground, say, he'd be straight over, yelling, 'What you doing to my brother?' Then boof! He'd punch them. Very protective and ready for a fight was Little Charlie! The two of them were very close – still are today – and would always have each other's backs.

And, of course, my husband loved seeing them do it. He had really enjoyed his days boxing, and was pleased that his passion was being passed on to the next generation. He got very involved and they would all sit together at night after they had been to training, discussing moves and how to improve. Charlie would also go to all the matches and cheer them on. It was a bit of a boys' bonding thing in our house.

Not that I didn't get involved too – I actually enjoyed going along to the odd match. Although I felt pretty guilty about it one time when I was watching Little Charlie in a fight. I was getting really into it, and kept shouting,

'Come on, boy. Give 'im one! Go on, smack him! Come on, boy!'

And this woman next to me eventually got all upset and said to me, 'That other boy you're talking about is my son!'

I felt really awful and just kept apologizing. I was still happy when Charlie won, though!

Stephen and Charlie kept it up for years after, until their heads got turned by drink, girls and football and they weren't prepared to put in the time training or fighting no more. And I remember Stephen got his nose broke, which put him off too.

In fact, boxing seems to be in my family's blood – on *The Only Way Is Essex*, my grandson Mark, Carol's son, used to do boxing. And he is seen having a boxing match for charity with another person on the show, Kirk Norcross, who he beats. He was good!

Stephen was having the odd drink by then – we knew 'cause we took him for his first pint! He looked older than his fourteen years, and I remember he came with us all dressed up with a blazer on to a pub down the road from our house. He went up and ordered and bought the drinks as well, and no one questioned his age. He had a pint of beer, and was very pleased with himself.

So to encourage the boys to drink more at home rather than going out where we had no idea what they were up to, we bought a king-sized snooker table. It was a great big thing, but we bought it 'cause we thought it would stop them getting in trouble. They were at that age when boys tend to get into fights and stuff, and me and Charlie wanted to stop our boys doing that. It wasn't that we didn't trust them not to get into trouble, but when they are just out hanging round the street corners, other people can easily start trouble with them like, for no reason.

Of course, they didn't spend all their evenings in there – a lot of the time they'd go to the pub first, but then at the end when it was closing, mostly they'd end up back at the house, and whoever came back would be behind the bar serving themselves. Sometimes they'd bring their own beer, or if we had some in, they'd have that.

And other times they used to bring their dads in too. They'd sit there and get sloshed together, as I think other parents liked the idea of this kind of controlled bar too, and then they got to spend some time together, fathers and sons. It wasn't always ideal – and sometimes it felt like we had just opened another pub! – but I would sooner have had that than Stephen and Charlie out to all hours, who knows where, and up to who knows what.

Sometimes it would get out of control, though. I'd end up going downstairs at the end of the night if it was still too rowdy, saying, 'Please, please, please can you all go home, and my boys go to bed. Don't play about no more 'cause I've got to get some sleep.' But it didn't always work. Can you believe there were days when people would come over and stay for two or three days at a time before I'd finally say enough was enough and they would leave! And I wonder why our house had a reputation as the party house . . .

FIFTEEN

Flying High

The mum-in-law's health had continued to deteriorate 'cause of her diabetes. She was still living with Joe in Bromley-by-Bow, but would spend a lot of time at ours, partly because she needed help with quite a few things that Joe wasn't really able to do. The biggest issue was her leg. The pains in it had got worse and worse, and she really struggled to walk or even stand on it, so basic stuff like cooking meals had become a real struggle for her.

Then in February 1975, I think it was, just after my Susan's sixteenth birthday, the mum-in-law was told she had got gangrene in her leg and she was going to need it chopped off if she was to survive. Well, she was horrified of course, but went in for the operation, I suppose 'cause she didn't really have no other choice. But she never come out. She had the operation, and they removed her leg from below her knee, but for whatever reason it didn't seem to go too well, so they kept her in the hospital and she just got worse. She was in there about two more weeks and then she died. It was like the shock of the operation, or of losing her leg, had killed her. She was in her sixties at the time, and these things can happen to people that age, but it was still awful.

I was sorry to lose her. She was a lovely lady, and we had spent a lot of time with her over the years. But I was also sorry she had gone for Charlie's sake. He loved his mum and was so close to her. He was really upset by it.

He talked to me a bit about what he was feeling but, in true Charlie style, he dealt with it by going out and getting drunk. Getting himself into a state where he wasn't able to think too much about what had happened to his mum was his main way of coping at the time, but I didn't realize what he was up to.

Now, I would realize it and think, 'Oh, he is trying to drown his sorrows,' and be supportive of him. But then I didn't get the link as I didn't know it was something that people did, and I used to say, 'What the bleedin' hell is the matter with you, going out and getting drunk?'

Then he'd sit there and have a little tear about his mum. And on the one hand I would feel bad for him, but on the other I admit I didn't. Obviously it was horrible what he was going through, but I would get all factual about it too, and be like, 'She's gone and that is it. You have to just get on.' And I would think about me and my mum and the fact I had lost her when I was so young, and part of me would think how I did feel bad for Charlie losing a parent, but at least he had had her for a long time – that was something I had never had.

But, I tell you, the spookiest thing happened a couple of days later. Charlie had explained to the children that their nanny had died, and they all seemed to deal with it privately, working it through in their own minds and in their own time.

Anyway, at the time Stephen and Little Charlie were still sleeping in the same room, what we called the box room, and shared bunk beds. Well, we were all in bed a couple of days after her death when the dog started barking downstairs. Like, not just the usual restless bark when he heard someone pass outside or something, but really going mad, barking like he was crazy. And Charlie got up to investigate, but he didn't get very far before he had to change direction and head to the boys' room.

'Cause all of a sudden the boys sat bolt upright in bed as they'd had the lives scared out of them – a drawer in their cupboards just suddenly shot out. Gospel. And the poor things were terrified and started screaming.

It might have been hanging out and just fallen if it

wasn't in properly, but the fact it was at the same time as the dog started going so crazy downstairs . . . Well, to this day we don't know why it happened, but Charlie went in and told the boys that it was their nan's way of saying goodbye, and that they shouldn't worry. I'm not sure that he reassured them, though – I remember Stephen later saying he wished she hadn't bothered with her goodbye, which made me laugh! But it was a very odd night.

And then, as if that weren't enough bad news for us, very soon after Uncle Joe died.

He had been in hospital at the same time as the mum-in-law because of bowel problems, which turned out to be cancer, and it wasn't long after he was diagnosed that it killed him.

I was there when he passed away. I was the only one there because his daughter lived abroad and his son was in the army. I remember I stayed with him in the hospital and held his hand and gave him a kiss, and he knew he was dying 'cause he said to me, 'Goodnight, Pat,' and then he went. I got the most terrible sensation when he passed away – it was like a puff that went right the way through me. I can still remember that feeling now, and yet I have been there when other people have died and never had the same thing. Innit funny how it can be such a different experience with different people?

I don't think we ever told him that me mum-in-law had died. But I do wonder if he knew deep down, and it was one of those occasions when two people are in love and don't want to carry on life without each other. He really did think the world of her and they were always together.

My dad, meantime, was still going strong, thank goodness. He would spend a lot of weekends at ours, relaxing with the kids or heading off to the pub for a pint with Charlie.

Then around 1976, I think it was, my dad said he had something serious to discuss. He sat me down at my kitchen table and looked all nervous. I had no idea what was coming, and started worrying, then he took a deep breath and said to me, 'Can I have your approval?'

'What for?' I asked. I remember not having a clue what he was going on about and feeling confused.

And he said, 'To get married.'

Can you believe that after more than twenty years of courting Bet, he had finally decided he wanted to get married to her? I had to laugh. I have no idea what made him suddenly decide that was the time. Maybe it just felt right. Or maybe, thinking about it, her husband had died. He had been in a mental hospital for years, and their marriage had effectively been over for a long time. But I suppose him dying would have freed her up to tie the knot with Dad. It wasn't for me to question, though.

I just said, 'Dad, you have been courting her for I don't know how long. You want to get married, you get married!'

Besides, over the years I had come to like her a lot more than I had as a teenager. She was a bit more genuine with me, and talked to me on more of an equal level. More like a friend.

I hadn't thought that when they first got together, though, for a couple of reasons. First, she came into Dad's life at a time when me and him were not getting on, mainly because I was dating Charlie by then and he didn't approve, and she sided with him and didn't help things. But I also felt horrified, and hurt, that he was courting again, and I needed more time after Mum's death to accept that he could be with another woman.

But by this time I was able to deal with it properly in my own mind, and see that them marrying was not him replacing Mum but just his way of moving on with his life. And, to be honest, Bet had stuck with him for so long and understood him so well, it kind of felt like that needed to be acknowledged in some way. Maybe that was his thinking when he decided it was time for marriage. Who knows?

So they did get married, and we went to the wedding

in Bow Road Registry Office. It was a nice, simple marriage ceremony and it was good to see how happy they were. Although no one could ever replace my mum, I was glad to see Dad content. He had a beaming smile plastered over his face the entire day, and it made me feel good to see just how happy he was.

By the mid-1970s it was all the rage to go on package holidays abroad. Not too far, mind – mainly Spain and the likes. Anyway, we were starting to hear a lot about them and thought we'd give it a try. I still loved my trips to the caravan, but I had never been abroad. Obviously Charlie had when he was in the navy, back when he was in his late teens. He pretty much went all the way around the world, even to Australia. But you don't see it properly when you are in the navy, as you are mostly just stuck in the port before you move on to the next place.

So when we booked a deal for me, Charlie and the two boys to go to Benidorm, it was something completely different for us – it was my first trip out of the country and the first time Charlie had ever been abroad for an actual holiday.

By then the three girls thought they were too old to be going on holiday with their parents – and probably couldn't wait to get the house to themselves. I used to say to whichever kids stayed at home when we were away – out of earshot of their father – if you are going to do anything, or have any parties or whatever, for God's sake, when we get home, make sure the place is clean. And they would always put on their best innocent faces and shake their heads and go, 'No, Mum! We would never do anything like that!'

Well, I will never know for sure, but I would bet my bottom dollar they had no end of parties. 'Specially Carol – she wouldn't have missed an opportunity to do something like that. I'd bet my life on her having parties while we were gone! But in all fairness, if they did, I will give them their dues that they did clean the place up afterwards.

Anyway, for our first holiday, Benidorm, on the south coast of Spain, seemed like the best option because some of our friends had already been there and recommended it and also 'cause we could get a package deal for not too much.

I didn't really know what to expect, either of the plane, as obviously I'd never flown, or of Benidorm itself. And, if I'm honest, I was afraid of going abroad. It wasn't like today – then it was a complete unknown. Growing up, it had been a big adventure to just go thirty miles to the coast, and this was a world away from that. People speaking a different language, different food, different temperatures . . .

Well, we went to get the plane from Gatwick Airport, I think it was. And the whole checking-in process was so much simpler than today. None of this no liquids or all that nonsense about things in plastic bags.

I remember getting on the plane and strapping myself into my seat, feeling completely petrified. Charlie was next to me, also completely terrified, saying prayers and crossing himself, which made me even worse as I wasn't used to seeing him openly frightened. He was normally the person I looked to for reassurance! And the boys were sat behind us. Little Charlie was especially excited as it was his birthday – his thirteenth, if I remember rightly.

As the plane taxied down the runway and took off, well, I had my eyes squeezed tight shut and was gripping onto the seat, but the boys weren't happy about that. They were determined I should be enjoying the experience. 'Innit good, Mum? Look out the window! You have to look!' they were saying. Oh, I could have killed them, but eventually I opened my eyes and took a peek. Just as I looked out the window, though, it seemed that we were coming back round on ourselves. Then the next thing the pilot made an announcement in this very posh English accent:

'I'm terribly sorry, but we have to land back at

Gatwick Airport due to a technical fault. There is absolutely nothing to worry about, though.'

Nothing to worry about? I don't bleedin' think so! As we came down on the runway, I could see out the window there was a fire engine following right behind us, and it was only once it had stopped and we were all off that they admitted, 'We are terribly sorry, but what actually happened is that one of the engines caught fire.'

Well, what do you think to that as a first experience of flying? I was totally and utterly terrified. I can tell you, there were a lot of people panicking after that. And it was an eleven-hour wait until the next plane was ready to take us on our holiday, though luckily they put us up in a hotel for that time. Some people didn't get back on as they were too scared after that, but we did as we decided it was a horrible one-off, and that we couldn't let the boys be disappointed at missing their holiday – or us!

Not that our troubles were over . . . Although the flight was a lot smoother this time, I can honestly say I kept my eyes closed most of the way. I only opened them as we landed in Benidorm, and my first impressions were not good. There were just high-rise buildings and tower blocks everywhere.

Then just as we got to the hotel and walked through into the reception area, a fight broke out amongst a group of lads. And when it ended one of the boys came over to me – I suppose they were waiting for the police to come – and he said, 'If I have to go to court, would you be able to bail me out?' I felt sorry for him as he had no parents with him, so I just said something vague like, 'Oh, we'll have to wait and see.' But in my head, I was saying, 'As if, mate!' My God, I was just thinking, 'What hell hole have we brought ourselves to?'

But, in fact, the rest of the trip wasn't too bad. The hotel was pretty basic but did us fine, and the food was all English anyway, so I didn't have to see if I could take to anything new. In true Charlie style, he turned his attention to the local bars and befriended all the young lads who spent their evenings in them, so he headed off with them and left me with the boys a lot of the time. But I didn't mind, and we kept ourselves well entertained at the beach, or I would relax by the pool while the boys messed around in the water.

Then, coming home, the important bit was the duty-free. I couldn't believe how much we could save buying cigarettes and alcohol at the airport, so we tried to get as much in our bags as possible! But sadly we didn't have space for a lot – a lesson learned for future holidays. From then on we would fly out with our cases practically empty, and come back with a hundred packets of fags, and as many bottles of spirits as could be squeezed in!

One thing I did decide after that holiday, though, was that I needed to learn to swim. I'd never liked being in the water much – I was always sure I would drown. It wasn't that I had had an 'specially bad experience. I think it was more just that I'd never learned to swim as we didn't have lessons at school or anything back in them days. And as I got older it seemed like it was too late as I was really afraid by then.

Though I made sure all the kids learned to swim. They all had lessons and had the certificates and all that. But I just never had the urge to join them in the pool. I couldn't bear any water near my eyes, and even when I used to try lying in the bath, just to get myself used to it, as soon as it came up near my neck, I'd jump up quick. I don't know why – it was just a reaction like I thought I'd drown. Oh, it's terrible, ain't it?

And the kids, who had tried their hardest all their lives to get me to swim, bless them, finally said to me, 'Mum, you can't go abroad if you can't swim.' And I decided they were right 'cause I had felt like I was missing out by not going in the pool or the sea on our holiday, so as soon as I got back, I finally signed up for some swimming lessons.

June got me going down to a swimming club on Loxford Lane in Ilford, where her daughter was having lessons, and I remember being terrified that first week.

But bit by bit the teachers built up my confidence and showed me how to do it.

Not that I ever became that fond of it – I still used to walk along the bottom of the pool while making the motions with my arms on the surface, telling the kids I was swimming! But in the end I got into it and became all right at it, and did so many lengths and all that that I could kind of call myself a swimmer. Enough that I could go on holiday and cool off in the pool or mess around with the kids in the sea if I wanted to, without panicking anyhow.

We got a taste for holidays abroad after Benidorm, and we went back to Spain a few more times, and Majorca – I liked it there. Then a whole group of us booked to go to Lloret de Mar on the south coast of Spain one year, us and another family, but the hotel got cancelled so we got sent to Tenerife instead.

But my favourite was a city in the south of Cyprus called Paphos, and, in fact, we fell in love with it so much that we went there thirteen years running! We kept going back to the same beautiful hotel and everything. It was just me and Charlie who went there, without the kids, and the hotel owner always knew to expect us. It got to the point where we didn't even need to book – he'd automatically have it in his diary. And one time he gave us an extra week for free on the end of our fort-night holiday.

'Are you doing anything next week? No? Well tell your children you are not coming back just yet! And it's on me.'

So we done that. Lovely man! I am more than happy to keep going to the same place each time when it is that good.

Not that I got any more happy about the actual flying. I was still frightened and always will be. I sit there with my seatbelt on, and no matter how much I am dying to go to the toilet, I won't get up. No way.

My husband's way of dealing with it was to get blind drunk beforehand. I remember we went on holiday once with friends, and both the men were absolutely para-lytic before we even got on the plane – they were prac-tically carried upstairs and on-board! You'd never get away with that these days. If you look at all merry, you've had it.

And, of course, the laws on smoking are different too. Back then we used to sit puffing away in our seats, just flicking the ash into an ashtray in the seat arm. Things haven't half changed.

SIXTEEN

Drama and Despair

All in all, things seemed to be ticking along pretty nicely. The family was doing well and we were happy and settled. But then, just because life seemed to be straightforward for once, it had to all fall apart, didn't it? And not once, but twice, in the strangest of ways.

First of all, Dad got some problems with his stomach. I forget what it was exactly, but it was causing him a fair bit of pain, so he had to go to hospital – St Andrew's as usual.

Me and Charlie were just back from holiday at the time – Spain, I think, or Cyprus – so we took him to the hospital, and then I remember we had to take his canary home with us to look after. He loved birds, did my dad, and he had a yellow canary called Joey at the time that was his pride and joy. So we agreed to feed it and look after it while he was in there.

Then a few days later we went back to the hospital to see him. I only really link it with the holiday 'cause I can remember looking over at Charlie in the car on the way there and he was really brown.

We had rushed in to make visiting hours and were sat talking to Dad, catching up on all our news, when Charlie said he didn't feel too good. He was all hot and sweaty, and kept complaining, 'Ain't it warm in here?' although I thought it was fine. So he said he was just going outside to get some fresh air. Well, next thing I know a nurse was gesturing frantically for someone down my end of the ward to come over to her. I was looking around to see who she meant, and she was like, 'No, you!' and pointing at me.

I went over and she said, 'Weren't you with a gentleman in here just before?' When I nodded, she continued, 'Well, I'm sorry to tell you, but he has collapsed outside so we have admitted him.'

Oh, my heart rightly went crazy, and I felt sick with panic, but I knew I had to keep it together. So I apologized to Dad and said I would be back, then raced off with her to find Charlie.

It turned out he had keeled over in the car park, and someone had spotted him and got help, so they saw to him straight away in the hospital. By the time they had got me upstairs to him, he was in a bed, now as pale as anything, his holiday tan all but disappeared, with drips seeming to go into him all over his body.

A doctor pulled me to one side and said, 'Sorry to tell you, Mrs Brooker, but your husband has had a heart attack. It was only a minor one, so he will be fine, but it was a heart attack all the same. So he needs a bit of time to recover, and we want to keep an eye on him to see it was just a one off.'

I couldn't believe what he was saying. My Charlie had had a heart attack – he was only forty-six so seemed much too young for that. But while it was anything but funny then, I've joked since that if he was going to have a heart attack, he couldn't have chosen a better place! At the time, though, I was at my wit's end. I had gone to the hospital to visit my sick dad, only to have my husband collapse, leaving me with two very ill patients on my hands. I was really quite worried and scared, but I've always found that the practical side of my mind kicks in in those kinds of situations, so I concentrated on things like making Charlie comfortable and being sure my dad was fed, rather than my fears.

So I spent the rest of the day up at the hospital with him, but being as people didn't have mobiles then, I had no way of contacting the kids to tell them where I was or what was happening. I used the hospital phone to call the house, but every time I tried, there was no one there to answer.

I started talking to another couple in there who had brought someone else in, telling them my difficulties, and when they left they very kindly offered to drive me home.

Luck would have it that as we were driving along over Canning Town Bridge in Bromley-by-Bow, dear Carol was going past in the other direction in an open top car with her boyfriend at the time, David Wright – yep, that's the right surname as she has dated more than one Wright! I started screaming and waving at her and managed to get her attention, and they pulled in round the corner.

I dashed over and said, 'Daddy's been took bad at the hospital! He collapsed,' and she was all confused, and like, 'What? I thought you went there to see granddad?!' So I had to explain what had happened and she went straight over there, while I went home to try to contact the other kids and get some things together.

So this kind couple drove me home, then the fella said to me, 'Tell ya what. We can see you are having an awful night and have a lot on your plate, so getting a taxi is going to be a bit of a nuisance. If you hurry up and do what you need to do, we'll drive you back to the hospital as well.'

It's nice people like them that make your life that bit easier at times like that.

But do you know what? When I got into the house I found yet another disaster – Dad's bleedin' canary had only gone and died. I went to feed it, and it was just lying there as stiff as anything on its back with its legs in the air!

But I got everything sorted and went back to the hospital for the rest of the night, and found that they'd taken Charlie to a ward upstairs from my dad.

So you can imagine what visiting hours were like for me. Every night I used to run in after I'd spent a day at work, and then been home to tend to the kids. First I'd go see my dad, then run up and see my husband. And even though they both had other visitors too, like Dad's wife Bet and the children, if I spent more time with Dad, Charlie used to moan, and if I spent more time with Charlie, my dad used to moan. And them days you only got an hour for visiting times – 7 to 8 p.m. to be exact. It wasn't like you could spend all day there, like you can today. So I had my work cut out keeping both grumpy, impatient men happy!

It got so daft that I asked the nurses if we could have the two of them in the same ward, side by side, then I could be like, 'Y'all right?' to one, and turn my head to see the other and say 'Y'all right?' without getting myself in trouble! Oh dear, we used to joke about it 'cause it was about all you could do, but can you imagine? I really was stretched to the limit.

Once Dad started getting a bit better, he was more mobile so he used to go up and visit Charlie in the day, which must have passed the time for them both a bit. Though I imagine the pair of them together were a right pain for the nurses.

The other thing I was doing, between visits and work, was going on the hunt for a yellow canary. I didn't want Dad to come out and find his bird was dead, so I decided to get a replacement and hope he wouldn't notice. Oh, I went everywhere to get that thing, I tell ya! And eventually I found one – although it cost me about three or four quid, which was still quite a bit of money – and I put it in the cage to replace the dead one.

Well, both my husband and my dad were got better and after a week or so Charlie was allowed out, followed by Dad a couple of days later. I tell you, that was a relief.

But the first thing Dad did when he got back to us was look in Joey's cage, and he did a double-take.

'Pat! That's not my bird now, is it?'

'Course it is, Dad.'

'No, no, I know my Joey, and that is not him.'

He was so sure that I had to 'fess up in the end, and I was rightly annoyed. I'd gone all over the place to get that bleedin' bird as perfect as could be, and really I could have got him any old bird, or any pet for that matter, but I thought it had to be this yellow canary – and I got it wrong.

After I told him, though, he laughed and went, 'I dunno why you bothered 'cause Joey was so old, he was, that I was expecting him to die any day really.'

Oh, the performance I had been through . . . I could have cried! But Dad took this new bird home anyhow, not that I think it lasted long.

But apart from the initial drama with the bird, everything went back to normal – at least with us. It was June's world that was turned upside down next. The husband who Charlie had tried to warn her off on her wedding day really had turned out to be the wrong choice as far as she was concerned. They had gone on to have a second baby, but let's just say the pair of them clashed, and things between them could get pretty heated. I know Charlie went round one time to have a word with her husband – but after three years of marriage she came to us and said it just wasn't working.

She had been so desperate for her freedom from her parents she hadn't taken any notice of what she was getting into.

So she moved back in with us, and, of course, we welcomed her home with open arms. After a while the council got him to leave their flat, and then June and the kids moved back in there. But she seemed to need us a lot more for quite some time after the break-up while she got herself back on her feet. She'd come and stay with us every Friday to Monday. That carried on until a couple of years later when she met a nice man called John and got married to him – and this time he was for keeps! He took Kelly and Dean on and loved them as though they were his own, and, as far as they were concerned he was their real dad. In fact, he adopted them.

We'd had an up and down few months, but 19 March 1980 was a day to celebrate, as me and Charlie had been married for twenty-five years! I couldn't believe how the time had passed, and how much we had gone through together. On the one hand it seemed to have flown, and on the other it was like we had been together for a thousand years!

Now, I had always liked the idea of renewing my wedding vows. I don't know why, I think I just thought it was a nice way to prove that you cared about the person just as much as you had the day you had married them – or more.

I don't agree with these ones who do it every year, mind. That is daft, and I wonder why you would want to do that – how many times do you need to prove to someone you love them?! But when you have gone through a hell of a lot together, it is just like a sign that you realize that – and are ready to tackle any other problems the world throws at you together as well.

But Charlie didn't agree with it at all. 'I done it once, and we have been together for all these years, why should I go and do it again?' he'd say whenever I brought it up. 'No, I love you, and I should be able to tell you that I love you now rather than waiting to do it in front of other people. Doesn't make no sense to me.'

When we reached our twenty-fifth wedding anniversary he told me he had a surprise for me, and for a minute I thought it might have been that – that he had arranged for us to renew our vows. But instead it was something with the same kind of thinking behind it, but more private to us. He bought me another wedding ring. It was gold with a kind of floral pattern etched into it. My original one was similar, gold with a pattern, but over the years it had worn down and the pattern had disappeared. By then it just looked like a gold band. So I put the new one on my wedding finger and swapped the old one to the same finger on my right hand.

He said, 'You have had that one for twenty-five years, and now you can have another one for another twenty-five years – let's hope anyhow!'

And me and Charlie went on holiday to Malta, just the two of us, and had a lovely time together. Then on our first night back, the kids said to us that they wanted to go out for an evening to celebrate with us. Well, I was all tired after the holiday and was saying, 'I don't really want to, I can't be bothered.' And everyone was like, 'No, Mum, you have to come.' So in the end I got dressed up and we went. I can't remember the venue exactly, I just remember it was in a basement.

And when we got there . . . well they had organized a whole surprise party for us. All our friends and family were there, and they had done the place up lovely. I felt guilty then for not having wanted to go, as they had made such an effort! And as it turned out we had a lot of fun and a really good evening. It was a true reminder of the great people we had around us in our life.

SEVENTEEN

The Circle of Life

The eighties got off to a bad start for two reasons. Firstly, we lost another important member of the Brooker family – our beloved dog Rex. He got really bad rheumatism, and could hardly walk or move at all in the end really. It got so that he spent most of the time just lying in his bed in the corner, and we were having to feed him like a baby. Even for him to go to the toilet we had to lift him up in a blanket and lift his back legs to get him to do a wee. And although everyone knew it was probably time to let him go, no one wanted to. But eventually the vet said that we were being cruel keeping him alive as he wasn't getting any quality of life. So I agreed that we had to do it, it had to happen, and we should let him be put down.

The whole family was really sad about it as he had been such a part of our lives while the kids were growing up, both in the pub and out in Essex. We had had him throughout his whole life from when he was just a little puppy, and I always felt safe with him. But while he had made a great guard dog and protector, he wouldn't have hurt a fly. He lived to be about thirteen years old, so he had a good run. If the kids had had their way, though, he would probably still be here today, just sat curled and unmoving in the corner!

Stephen and June took him to the vet's to be put down, and I know they found it really hard. We all did. And that's when I vowed that I'd never have any more dogs as losing him was just too hard – I was so attached to him. But I do quite often look after other people's dogs, so I still have contact with them. Just not my own – I have lost enough people and animals, thank you very much.

Then the other bad thing that happened at the start of the 1980s was Charlie losing his driving licence for a year. As I said before, he wasn't keen on the no drinking and driving rule when it was introduced, and he wasn't very good at sticking to it! I suppose it was always going to happen that he would get caught one day.

Sure enough, he was stopped one night, and pretty much fell out of the car at the policeman's feet. It was a horrible time really. Charlie felt a bit stranded without the car, and it upset him a fair bit. He also worried about the impact it would have on his ability to work and support the family – the boys were still at home at this time – but he had actually stopped the meat deliveries and cabbing by that point and was able to adapt the insurance work around it, so it wasn't so bad.

Meantime, the girls were all moving on and starting to create their own families. It seemed to happen in age order, with them moving out one by one. Carol had met a fella called Mark Wright on a night out at the White Hart pub on Bethnal Green Road. His dad owned the pub, as well as several others in the area, and Mark was an East End lad through and through. They got married on 13 Aug 1983.

But we always made a point of spending a lot of time together as a family, and still had everyone around all the time, 'specially for Sunday lunch. In fact, our Sunday lunches became somewhat famous!

It also became a tradition for Charlie and the kids to go off for a bit of a trip to the pub on a Sunday. They would be joined by my dad, and any other friends/ boyfriends/girlfriends who were around at the time. They'd get there for midday just as the doors opened, and then it was like they were speed drinking. The pub was only open for two hours and, believe me, they made the most of it.

Then they came home, where I'd have been while they were out, preparing the food.

And I tell you, I often found myself having to feed upwards of a dozen people, often close to twenty. Now, I'd like to think it was 'cause my cooking was so good, but a lot of the time I think it was just 'cause our house was known as the social one – and they probably couldn't be bothered to cook for themselves neither!

It felt a bit like bedlam at times, but it was a good social occasion, and Charlie and Dad would be holding court at the table. Dad really came into his own at times like that and was a great character, the real life and soul of it. And him and Charlie were both really funny and would bounce off each other, keeping everyone entertained.

Then after we had eaten, the girls would clear up and have our own chat sat on the big sofa in the lounge, while the men would sit and have a few games of cards. From what I got told, a fair few quid would change hands, but they'd be having a great time. Not that I was that keen as sometimes I thought they were getting carried away with themselves – sometimes they would start playing at 4 p.m. on the Sunday and finish in the early hours of Monday morning!

I always remember the Christmases we used to have, when the number at the table swelled even more – I'm sure every one of my kids seemed to invite their whole social circle to join us! But it was great. There was always a real strong family feel.

In May 1987, we had a particularly busy time of it. First, Susan gave birth to a son who she called Stephen. Her baby was born on a Thursday.

Then my son Stephen got married two days later on the Saturday. He married a girl called Lynne and Susan's daughter Danielle was a bridesmaid. Susan had only come out of hospital on the Friday night, and she wanted to see her daughter in action, as well as her brother tie the knot. So she came down for a bit, having left baby Stephen with friends – but couldn't stay for long, as Stephen had jaundice and she needed to rush back to him. It was all go, I tell you!

Well, my dad was at the wedding, and from what I could see he was having a really good day. He was seventy-six at the time, but that didn't stop him joining in with everyone and the action.

All the men went for a few drinks beforehand, and he joined them then. So much so, in fact, that Stephen later said while he was waiting for Lynne to come down the aisle, he heard my dad say to Charlie, 'I wish they'd hurry up, I'm busting for a piss!' It definitely gave Stephen a laugh and calmed his nerves.

Then at the reception I can still remember him getting

up and dancing, and smiling away as he joined in with it all.

But sadly that was the last big family occasion we would all have together.

Dad was staying with us that weekend in Chudleigh Crescent, and he kept saying to me, 'I can't go to the toilet, Pat'. Dad always swore blind that a beer a day would make him go to the toilet. I've no idea if there is truth to that or if it was just an old saying of his, but he stuck to it. So I said, 'You've had plenty of beer this weekend, haven't you, Dad? Are you sure?'

And he said he had, but he was sure, so we got him to the doctor's on the Monday. Well, he had to go back the following week for an x-ray, and then they discovered he had bowel cancer and he had to go into hospital. With Uncle Joe having died of it, I guess it runs in the family.

Just two weeks later, while Stephen and Lynne were still on honeymoon in Minorca, Dad went in for what we hoped would be a minor operation to sort it out. But it turned out it was much more serious than we had first thought, and he went downhill very quickly. Just like the mum-in-law had done when she went in, Dad never came out of hospital.

He ended up hooked up to these machines that were keeping him alive, and then they told me there wasn't anything more they could do and they would have to turn the machine off. My brother and our kids all went in to say goodbye, and then we had to leave the room so they could do it.

It was horrible. Me and Dad had had our ups and downs when I was a teenager after Mum died, and then he hadn't talked to me for a few years after I married Charlie, as he had disapproved. But once we had been reunited, we had had a really good relationship and his death seemed to leave a real hole in my life. It also meant that now, I suppose, I was officially an orphan.

I had all sorts of mixed emotions running through me. Within less than a month I had had a birth, a marriage and a death. It was a difficult period, and I didn't know what to feel a lot of the time. I would sit and cry about Dad, sad that I would never see him again, then I'd remember the new members of my family and smile. It was like a reminder of the way life just keeps on going and changing, and you just have to accept it. So, as ever, I just put my head down and got on with life.

I think my dad dying was the first time the kids, or at least the boys, had experienced the shock of someone close to them dying. They had been too young to really understand or be that deeply upset when Charlie's mum had died, but this time it was different. I know Stephen took it 'specially badly. Perhaps partly 'cause he was also going through mixed emotions – he had just got married so on the one hand it was one of the happiest times of his life, but on the other, he was grieving over the loss of his granddad.

One thing I did do to try to distract myself straight after Dad died, though, was to go on holiday to Orlando. Carol and her family had already gone out there for a break, and they kept telling us to come and join them, but I always said, 'No, I can't. I couldn't travel that far.'

But eventually Charlie said to me, 'You know what? Your dad's left us a couple of bob. Why don't we use that and go out there and have a good time?' So that's what we did. We booked a plane to Florida and I loved it. I thought it was great and just what I needed to help me move on from what had been one of the most emotionally difficult times of my life.

EIGHTEEN

A Turn For the Worse

By the early nineties all the kids had moved out and on with their own families. Not that any of them had moved very far, 'specially Little Charlie, who was in the next road to us! Him and his wife Tracey had got a place in Tavistock Gardens, and can you believe there was only one garden dividing ours from his!

So on a sunny day, if Big Charlie was out in the garden and he could hear voices coming from Little Charlie's garden, he'd start shouting, 'Charlie! Who you got over?'

'Is that you, Dad?' would come back. 'It's so and so, and so and so, and we're having a barbecue.'

'Right, me and your mother are coming over!'

Even now that we were older, he wasn't one to be missing out on a party or any of the action.

Little Charlie had become the same – the older he

got, the more I could see he was my husband to a T. It is quite incredible how similar he looked to a young Charlie – and how much he behaved like him.

The boys had also discovered an old hobby of their dad's by then – beanos! On the one hand they hadn't changed – they were still called beanos, and involved coach-loads of lads heading to the seaside with crates of beer and sandwiches, then arriving at Margate or wherever they were going and heading off around the coast like lunatics. Then they'd head back to the bus late afternoon to make their way home. I remember Stephen once saying it was like an episode of *Only Fools and Horses*, and I know exactly what he meant!

But problems were starting to appear with them. If there are ten coach-loads of drunken men arriving in a town, at some point you are going to have a punch-up. So some of the coastal towns started putting an ex-clusion zone on coaches, and really that was the end of beanos. It was a shame – it makes you feel like people have become less civilized or something. But I think many a man got good enjoyment out of beanos while they lasted.

The number of grandkids I have seemed to be growing all the time at this point as well. And I am pleased to say that a lot of them inherited my ginger hair! Not that they were so pleased about it. While in my day at school you didn't get any hassle for it – it was only my freckles I got teased about – they seemed to get a hard time over it, which I never liked to see.

And, of course, I ended up as babysitter for them an awful lot of the time. All my kids were more than happy to leave the children with me for the evening so they could head out, not that I minded as I love spending time with all my grandkids. In total, June has three children, Susan has three, Carol has four, Charlie has two, and Stephen has two, so I had the potential of looking after up to fourteen children! Carol was the worst for it, though.

'Here, Mum, me and Mark are just off out. You don't mind having the kids for a few hours, do you?' she'd ask, having already made her plans, knowing full well I wouldn't say no! She would drop her three, Josh, Jess and Mark, off with me, and I'd leave them to play, or watch television, and then I'd get them fed and off to bed. They were quite well behaved, although sometimes Mark in particular would play up. But I'd holler at him or smack him if he did, and he soon behaved!

In 1995 I turned sixty years old, which as well as being a scary landmark, meant I had to retire from my role as dinner lady. I had stayed in my same role running the kitchen all that time, and seen some right changes to it too.

Sadly, the food had changed with the times and was less the kind of food I agreed with feeding kids. So the fresh meat and veg, all prepared and cooked by hand, had been replaced with what were almost ready meals – frozen pizzas, chips, chicken nuggets and the likes.

And it was no longer a case of paying 10 pence per meal, regardless of what you ate – now everything was priced differently. So say chips were 50p, beans were 30p, etc, each kid could end up paying anything between £1 and £2, which I thought had just made things over-complicated. But those were changes that were happening all over the country, and I had no say in it.

Regardless of the way things were heading, I was really sad to go. I was, as I still loved being in there on a day-to-day basis. And they weren't going to let me go quietly either! No. In fact, I got presented with an award from the mayor for my service to the school – I had been there twenty-six years!

It had been that long that in some cases I had even served two generations of the same family. Some of the children I had fed back when I had started work there had left and gone on through senior school, got married and had their own children – and then sent them to South Park Primary School too! And that was lovely. I liked thinking I had fed that many people over the years.

It meant that I knew half the people in the street

around us near Chudleigh Crescent too. So whenever I was out there would always be some child or another going, 'Miss! Miss!', bemused at running into me out of school and uniform. I always enjoyed seeing them.

So this award was given to me in a presentation, along with a big bunch of flowers, and then I had go right the way through the school with all the kids singing and going 'aahh!' It was even written about in the local paper! It was embarrassing as I don't like being centre of attention, but at the same time it was really nice. It felt good to be appreciated, and I had enjoyed my time as a dinner lady.

I was right sad to have to leave, though. I had some great years in that school – if it hadn't have been for the law making me retire, I would have stayed on another ten years! If it had been more like today, when it seems you can work till you drop down dead, I might have been fine, but then, no, it was a very strict rule that you had to retire by sixty.

And Charlie, who was sixty-five by then, also had to retire from his insurance work, as the cut-off point for men was sixty-five. It was good that we both called it a day at the same time so we could enjoy our retirement together, on the little pension money we got, combined with our savings. I was getting £40 a month at the time from my dinner-lady pension, and Charlie got a pension from the Co-op. Then we both had money from our old-age pensions, but that was only a small amount. You do better from it today.

Then one sunny weekend we were down staying in Clacton-on-Sea – it was 1996, I think, and we had just been retired for a few months and were getting used to the free time. Clacton-on-Sea is a town on the coast of Essex that used to be a pretty popular holiday destination. I'm not so sure as it is now, with everyone getting package holidays abroad and that, but back in the day it was one of the main places to go on holiday for English folks.

Well, this one time we were down visiting my daughter June for Easter, as she and her husband had a house there in a bit called Martello Bay. Years before, Butlins had been built on the site, with rows and rows of these little bungalow-type things where guests would stay. But by this time it had been knocked down and they were building a new housing development on top of it, which is where June and her husband John had just moved into.

Now that we were retired, we were wondering what to do with ourselves – if we should stay in the family home in Chudleigh Crescent or move to a new place. We had been talking about the fact that our house in Ilford was too big for just me and Charlie now all the children had moved out. It wanted a lot doing to it to repair it and, as my husband said, it would have cost us more than it was worth to have done it. But at the same time we loved the place, so it was hard to decide to leave it. So we hadn't really discussed what we were going to do. We had just discussed some ideas in passing.

Anyway, this one afternoon we were all sat in June's front room when suddenly my husband upped and disappeared off across the road to this new housing development, and he was gone for ages. Turned out afterwards that he had been in there asking the owners whether they could do this and that to a bungalow on a plot right across the road from June's 'cause, if so, he wanted it.

Well, the next thing I knew, he came back and said, 'I've laid down a deposit on a place.'

'You what?' I was stunned.

'Yeah. We need to move, and it'll be lovely down here in summer. Look, we have the sea just by the house!'

And that was it. Oh, I was mad. I knew in the end Charlie would have made the decision of where we went, but I couldn't believe he had done it without consulting me. But there was no point putting up a fight about it as the money was already part spent, so I just accepted it. We packed up the Ilford home and sold it, and moved out to Clacton. I wasn't half sorry to see our place in Chudleigh Crescent go, to be quite honest.

Looking back, I am sorry I ever left it now. It was lovely because all the kids and all the grandkids had been in there – all the little 'uns had been a part of that house.

But we did move and Charlie was right. The beach was right by our bungalow, and it would have been lovely – if we ever had a summer. The most we ever saw of it was about three weeks a year, I'd say. And the rest of the time . . . well, it was miserable. Living there was the worst thing I could think of.

As I said, Clacton wasn't the buzzing, lively holiday destination by then that it had been years before. It still has a pier and amusement arcades and the like, but it had become pretty much filled with retirement homes. And while me and Charlie were just reaching that age, it didn't mean we wanted to sit around wasting away, waiting for the last bit of our lives to play out.

Don't get me wrong, we still had some good times down there, just not on the scale Charlie had obviously imagined when he bought the bungalow. Most days June would drop us off at the swimming pool on her way to work. Now, I'll be honest, despite my lessons, I still couldn't really swim so well, so I'd potter about in the shallow end, doing a few strokes, and going back and forth doing widths – I never went to the deep end, though. No, thank you!

But Charlie was a good swimmer so he would be going for it, up and down on his lengths. His swimming was the main reason we were there really – he was trying to diet as he had put on a fair bit of weight over the years and knew it wasn't good for his health, so we had started the exercise with the idea that it would help him lose some. But much as we enjoyed the sessions in the pool, I can't say as it made much difference to his weight.

Then after June finished work – she was a care worker for elderly people – me and her might head into town and get a bit of food, or run any errands that we needed to do.

Of an evening me and Charlie had also joined a working men's club in Clacton. Leaving Ilford didn't mean I had managed to get Charlie away from that life-long habit of drinking and socializing! So he would go down there a lot, and sometimes I joined him.

But other than that, there wasn't a lot to do. I was so bored I even took to riding a bike around! I had ridden one before in my days as a dinner lady, so I borrowed one from June and I was ready to go. It was not a good place if you didn't have a car, and the bike became my way of getting about. I suppose it was also a good way of keeping fit.

I also missed being close to the rest of the family. I was so used to everyone just popping round that our new house seemed a bit empty. In the summer they would come down a fair bit, but over the winter we hardly saw them at all, which was a shame and was one of the biggest downsides to Clacton.

The only thing I did appreciate about the move to Clacton was the money it had saved us by downsizing our home. I had finally started to get stricter with myself over money. That might sound strange as I've always been good with it on one level. But that was partly because Charlie told me to, rather than because I believed I needed to be. But after the kids left and I no longer had them asking me for things, I got better at working out what we really needed. Rather than having Carol or whoever asking me for a pair of shoes, and me giving in and going, 'OK, I'll go and buy them, and I'll get you this and that as well,' I was more careful with money. It sounds silly, I suppose, but that was the point when I changed a bit. When Charlie tried to get me to think for myself.

Shortly after we moved to Clacton, though, Charlie began to get a bit sick. He was coughing a lot, and even started to bring up blood. We went to Colchester Hospital and he was in and out of there for a good while after, while they kept an eye on him and tried to work out what was going on with him. The doctor told him to give up smoking or he wouldn't live to see another year, so he did that. At the time he was smoking about thirty a day, mostly roll-ups. I smoked too, but nowhere near as many, more just the odd one here and there. I smoked John Player Specials – although a couple of times when I didn't have any I would sneak Charlie's tobacco pouch and try and roll one for myself, but every time the tobacco just fell straight out! So I left the roll-ups to him.

At that time, you could smoke pretty much anywhere, so you thought nothing of lighting up any time of day, no matter where you were. But once Charlie set his mind to giving up, he gave up just like that. When Charlie wanted to do something, there was no fussing around it – he would have the mental strength to just do it.

But other times the doctors would say it was nothing to do with smoking, and would give different reasons. It seemed that no one really knew the cause. But finally they decided that the air in Clacton wasn't doing him any good.

Well, that came as a surprise to me. Everyone had been saying that being down there should sort his lungs out – good sea air and all that. But the doctor said that actually it was bringing out lots of the problems with his lungs – which was something I could never really get my head around.

Anyway, we stuck it out there for five years, but we kept saying we needed to move back closer to London. And June and John were getting tired of it too. It wasn't the right place for them as they were quickly realizing. They were bored and had been struggling to find work as there wasn't much around there. So he would have to travel up to London on a Monday, work and stay with his mum while he did it, and then just go back to Clacton for the weekend. It wasn't the way for a couple to live really. It wasn't the time and place for them. So they moved back towards London, to Dagenham.

At the same time Charlie's hospital visits were getting more frequent and he would be in there for days at a time, so I was often at home on my own. I would go and visit him, but it would cost me £18 each way in taxi fares, every time, and I was getting pretty fed up with it all.

The girls kept telling me to move back to London as I couldn't carry on like that. Then Colchester Hospital said they were going to move him to a different hospital to get him better treatment, and they settled on Brompton Hospital, which is even closer to London than Colchester.

So in the end I said to Charlie, 'I can't go all that way every day. That's in London and I'm here, so I'm going to try and move back, and the girls think it's a good idea.'

And he agreed too, so I put the bungalow up for sale and started looking for somewhere closer to London.

And, I'll be honest, we obviously weren't the only people who didn't love it in Clacton. We have stayed in touch with a couple of neighbours who stayed there and send us a card every year, but they seem to be the only ones. Each year they tell us our old bungalow is up for sale again this year. Looks like that place can't keep anyone!

But anyway, while I was looking for a new place, the first place I tried was – can you believe – back in Chudleigh Crescent. But, of course, by then they were wanting twice what we had sold our place for, so there was no way I could have afforded that.

Well, I kept looking, and my kids helped me out and we would drive around and see different estate agents, but I wasn't having much luck. But then one of them got in touch with me and said that she was looking after some new houses being built in Dagenham that were specifically for wheelchair users, with wider doors and all that business, and by that time Charlie was so ill it looked as though he was going to be in a wheelchair for a while as he was struggling to walk.

I went and took a look at one of them, and although I have never thought Dagenham was the best area, I liked the house and it made sense for what we needed and where we needed to be. It was a three-bedroom house with a garden and was just the right size to suit us, so we took it. And actually, like I say, although Dagenham was never our choice, I don't actually have any complaints about it.

It is further out from the centre of London than any of our old East End homes – about twelve miles from the centre, I reckon – but it is still like a London suburb and is within the M25. The hospital was close by too, and all my kids had settled with their families within the area and I wanted to be back in a home where they were all nearby. Something I would never want to do is move too far to be able to visit them all easily. While they all might have moved on to do their own things, family then was as important to us as ever. Moving away from my lot is something I never want to do again.

NINETEEN

In Sickness and in Health

Once we were in Dagenham, Charlie's health just kept deteriorating. He was coughing a lot and struggling to breathe that easily, and he was still in and out of Brompton Hospital all the time. I lost track of how often he was back there. They sent him to Queen's Hospital for a bit too, which had recently been opened in Romford. Then there was the Royal London Hospital, in Whitechapel. Oh, they kept sending him to different hospitals. I think he tried all the ones in the city in the end! It seemed like they were struggling to find out the reason his breathing was so bad, so we were backwards and forwards all the time.

Then one day we were out on a few errands, and Charlie was driving. We were just off a road in Dagenham called Heathway and I had to run and do something, so I got him to pull up in this turning bit where people parked quite a lot, and said, 'You wait there while I just run across the road. I won't be a minute.' And he went, 'All right,' and stayed there with the engine running.

Well, when I came back, I turned the corner and saw there were people all round the car. I could feel myself panicking and started running towards the car, grabbing a man by the shoulder to ask him what had happened.

He said, 'Your husband's just had a crash but he don't know how. He's gone into a wall, but he don't realize what he's done.'

It wasn't a big crash – he was fine and all he'd done was a little bit of damage to the car. But he seemed dazed by it all, and had obviously taken it badly.

I really didn't know what to do, so I phoned up Little Charlie straight away and went, 'Quick, Chaz, you better get round here. Something has happened with your father.'

Well, he shot over at a million miles an hour to check on us and get the car sorted.

Meantime, a nice man nearby got Charlie a seat in his back garden and gave him a drink.

From what I could work out afterwards, Charlie had had a coughing fit and blacked out for a bit, with his foot hitting the accelerator. So actually it was quite lucky that all he had driven into was a brick wall. It could have been much worse.

But it was like that was the start of him taking a downward turn. From then onwards the hospital visits became more frequent, with us making endless trips to Brompton Hospital. Oh, it's a deadly place in there. The hours I spent sitting and waiting in that place . . .

Then he was diagnosed diabetic. It wasn't completely out of the blue, what with his mother having suffered from it as well. In fact, around the same time we'd also heard through the grapevine that Charlie's older brother Dickie had become diabetic. Sadly, Charlie had lost contact with Dickie after he married – there had been some kind of fall-out with his wife, I think, though I can't remember what. But it was a real shame 'cause the two boys had been so close when they were younger. Dickie had even been Charlie's best man at our wedding!

But we'd heard from someone that his diabetes had become so bad that he had got gangrene in his leg and, like his mother, had had to have it taken off. We didn't even know where he was living so didn't know how to get in touch. It was very sad, and then later we heard that he had died. The news only ever came through word-of-mouth as it were, which was a real shame.

Anyway, then Charlie was also diagnosed with COPD – chronic obstructive pulmonary disease, or sometimes it is called emphysema – which seemed to mean he had trouble everywhere – his kidneys, his heart and his lungs.

Ironically, the one place that seemed fine, despite all the troubles it had caused him in earlier years, was his stomach.

As to why he had developed COPD, well, I never really knew. Sometimes the doctors said it was down to him having smoked previously. But other times they said it was caused by asbestos 'cause Charlie had worked in a place with it when he was younger and doing decorating, before I had known him. They said it could have got into his lungs, but no one knew it was doing damage until years later.

Whatever the cause, though, it was not good news – we were told it was terminal. Everything that was going on in his body meant that it was a definite he wouldn't live to see it through. His doctor said it would be lucky if he lived a matter of months more, and that he would never live for a year.

Oh, I was devastated. I couldn't imagine life without Charlie around, and although you know it will happen one day, that one of you goes before the other, I was not ready for it to happen. And clearly nor was he. 'Those doctors don't know me, girl,' he'd say. 'You won't be getting rid of me that easily. I'm a lot tougher than they realize!'

And true enough, he was right. There was no way Charlie was going to do what was expected of him – he was far too stubborn for that! So what did he do? Made sure he lived another seven years!

But over those years Charlie become less and less mobile. We got him a wheelchair to get around when we were out and about, but to get him up the stairs I would have to be behind him, half supporting him and half pushing him. But because he wasn't able to be active, he was putting on weight and it was getting harder. He had always been a big fella, but this was more than that – at his heaviest he was twenty-two stone. And can you imagine little tiny me trying to move him around? At that time I weighed about nine stone, so less than half of him.

Well, we decided we needed to get a stairlift put into the house, so I asked someone from the council to come round and have a look and see what they could do. So this woman come round, 'Oh, it's a lovely house,' she said. 'Is it your house?'

'Yeah, yeah, we bought it ourselves.'

'Ah, right. See if you were on benefits, I could help you with the cost of the stairlift, but as it stands . . . I'm afraid you will have to pay for it yourselves.'

You what? Oh, that made me angry. I fought with the council for two years over it, before I realized I was never going to win and ended up paying nearly £3,000 to have a company come and put it all in for us.

Then, as Charlie got worse, he could hardly move to even wash himself in the shower, so I went back to the council and again asked for help, this time with getting a specially adapted shower with a seat and a handle.

'Oh, if only you were on benefits, we could help.'

It made me so angry. So if we gave up the house and got a council house and applied for benefits, they would help us? The system seemed so wrong. When Maggie Thatcher was in power she told people to buy their own house and that they'd be all right afterwards. And we'd done that, but it seemed to be backfiring on us – you are better off on benefits. I used to say to Charlie, 'We don't get nothing, do we, Charlie?' But as my husband always replied, 'We do, Pat. We have worked and looked after ourselves all our lives so we still have our self-respect.' And it was true.

Anyway, again it was another £3,000 of our own money for the shower. And I had to give Charlie a hand in the shower as he couldn't move to do it himself – he couldn't really do anything by then. I'd put on my swimming costume and jump in the shower with him and give him a wash down.

I'll tell you what, though, he was so proud that he wasn't willing to give me a break from it. I did ask to have some help at home, but again I was told I'd have to pay for it, so I just thought, 'I'll do it myself, don't bother.'

But there was a nurse from Brompton Hospital who used to come over every week or two to check in on Charlie and see that everything was all right. And she'd ask, 'Charlie, how's everything going? How about Pat? Can we send her away for a week for a break?'

But he was determined he didn't want a stranger looking after him. So he'd tell her, 'No, no, she'll help me, she'll look after me.' And that was that. I did.

He didn't take what I was doing for granted, though. Sometimes he would suddenly say to me, 'If it wasn't for you girl, where would we be?'

And I'd be secretly pleased to hear him acknowledge what I was doing, but wouldn't let on, taking the chance instead to try my luck for a day or so's break. 'Well, let other people help you out sometimes then!' I'd say, thinking how utterly exhausted I was.

'No, I married you, so you gotta help me.'

It was never any use. That was the way he was, and I had to laugh about it really.

The only time that I really left Charlie alone was when the girls sometimes came round and asked his permission to give me a bit of a break. They'd say, 'Dad, is it all right if we take Mum shopping for the afternoon?' and if he agreed, we would go to Lakeside – a big shopping centre nearby.

The boys would come around and sit with him while I was gone, but he was never happy about it. And I'd no sooner be gone than he'd start asking them, 'Where's your mother?' and a bit after that I'd get a call from him. 'When are you coming home?' he'd ask. Oh dear. But it was just one of those things.

His breathing had become so bad that there was talk of him going into care, but we weren't having that. There was no way Charlie wasn't going to stay in his own home. But he needed oxygen twenty-four hours a day so we got an oxygen machine installed in the house. We had this big box out in the passageway that had piping through to the rooms, and I would hook it up to whichever room we were in. Then there was piping to a mask that he would put on, which had these bits that went up his nose. It wasn't the most convenient thing but it meant that he was able to keep living at home. He also had these cylinders of oxygen that he would take with him if we ever went out. Not that he did go out much. I tried to get him out, and the boys tried too, but he couldn't really walk very well, and in the end I think it was such effort that he didn't end up enjoying it that much anyway.

We still had plenty of visits from the family, so we

stayed as close to them as ever. But there was one thing Charlie did take issue with, which was the way things were changing in terms of having children. He felt very strongly that it should all still be done in a traditional way – get married first and then have children. He thought that was what made a strong, tight family and so he was very against any of our grandchildren, who were starting to have their own children, doing so out of wedlock.

I tried saying to him, 'Charlie, this is how they do things these days. This is how kids today get on, so don't be like that.'

But he was determined and said he didn't care – he knew how things should be, and what his morals were, and that was that.

I'm quite traditional too and prefer things to be done how they always were, but I know that is the way of the world now so I try not to pass any judgement on it. Everyone does things in their own way.

But I was just glad that Charlie was still as opinionated and clear in his mind as ever, because while his body was failing on him, it was still the same Charlie that I was talking to and looking after every day.

The only thing in his mind that wasn't so good was his memory. So say we went to the hospital and they asked his date of birth, it might slip his mind for a minute and he'd get agitated and point at me, 'She knows. Tell them it, Pat.' And I'd calm him down and say it was 13 April 1930. I knew it off by heart – partly because Charlie used to joke it was an unlucky day for the world when he was born and I used to think, well, it was a lucky day for me!

Back at home, my daily routine was to get up at 6 a.m. every morning, get Charlie a cup of tea and a couple of biscuits, then give him his first lot of tablets. He was on such a lot of different tablets that it was almost a full-time job just counting them out and keeping an eye on them.

Then it was time to get him ready for the day, so shower, toilet – he was using a catheter by then, which I would change for him – and dressed. After that, at 11 o'clock, it was time for something to eat and the next lot of tablets. Then at different points throughout the day I had to inject him with insulin for his diabetes.

Charlie would spend a lot of time in his chair in the front room watching the television, and he would eat there on a tray, while I sat in another chair with my dinner on my lap too.

And that is how the day used to go on, right up until 10 p.m. when we'd go to bed. I suggested to Charlie that we get him a special remote-controlled bed that goes up and down with a memory foam mattress so that he was more comfortable and could get up easily when he was coughing. And when he ordered it, he said, 'This is a single bed. What about you? Don't you need one too?'

'Oh, don't worry about me,' I replied. 'I'll sleep anywhere, me!'

But he wasn't having that, and next thing I knew he had ordered me one too, and had them put in the same room so were both asleep in them next to each other!

I remember lying there night after night, thinking, 'Thank God for that,' that we had got through another day. Then I'd be straight to sleep to recover ready for the next day.

We had some light relief in March 2005, though – it was mine and Charlie's fiftieth wedding anniversary. The kids sorted us a party at the Prince Regent's Room in Loughton and arranged for a limo to take us there, which was a lovely touch! We felt right important going through Essex to the venue.

All our family and friends were there, and I have to say it was quite a boisterous affair, even for Charlie! Because despite being on oxygen and struggling to move or breathe a lot of the time, after he'd had a few whiskies some music came on that he liked so he got up and started dancing!

It showed just what a good night out with the family could do . . . or a bit of alcohol!

But things with Charlie continued to get worse and worse. I must have been up and down the hospital every other week with him. It was tiring, but that was how it was. He started to lose his balance because of his weight and everything else going on with him physically, and eventually he had a fall. I can't remember the exact details, but we called for an ambulance and they took him away to hospital. I remember the doctor telling me that this was only the start of it, that he was gonna keep falling over and collapsing and all that. It just seemed like one thing after another.

It was a horrible feeling, watching someone I loved slowly deteriorate before my eyes, and knowing the most I could do was ease things for him – I could never actually change or reverse what was happening.

And yeah, if I stopped and thought about it, of course it was draining. But I used to think, 'What's the good in worrying, or crying, or showing off about it? I have to do it and that's it!'

My girls used to say to me, 'Mum, I couldn't do what you are doing.' But I'd say, 'Oh, for Christ's sake, if I don't do it, who is going to? You won't do it, the doctors and nurses won't do it. Other people mightn't be bothered doing it, but that's not me.'

To me, I was his wife and it's what he needed, so I was doing it. I can't say it was the easiest time of my life, but I just got on with it. He was my husband and we had promised to look after each other for life when we got married, and that was me sticking to my word. I'm not sure so many people these days would do that, but in our day that is what marriage meant.

Then in June 2007 Carol came round to see us. As a diabetic Charlie needed to have his toenails clipped – you weren't supposed to do it yourself. It is something to do with what happens to your blood flow when you are diabetic, which means a lot of people have trouble with their feet and can end up, as with Charlie's mother, having one amputated.

Carol called up the NHS and asked them to come round to sort out his toenails. But they said they couldn't come to him – he had to go to them. She tried to tell them he could hardly breathe, and how hard it would be to get him there, but they insisted.

So we went to the surgery, and he couldn't even breathe coming out of the house. He struggled to breathe the whole way there, and was really bad by the time they got him into the chair. It was heartbreaking. And then when they cut his toenails this black blood started coming out. It was really scary.

Carol was so upset, but felt really angry as well. She went into the office and told the woman, 'Do you not understand? My Dad is dying. Yet you will not come to his house, and give him the comfort of just cutting his nails in his own home. You have forced him to come here. Can you not see the state he is in?'

The woman realized by then how bad it was and promised she would sort a home visit for the next time. But Carol walked out that day in tears, just thinking, 'Oh my God, he is going to die.' I think that was when it hit her just how bad he was.

I never allowed myself to think like that, though.

But then the next week it was early on a Wednesday morning, and he was sat downstairs. I was in another room, and Charlie stood up to do something. But he lost his balance and fell forward, landing on a glass coffee table we had in the room. He smashed his head on it quite badly, and bruising came up instantly.

I heard him and rushed into the room, then I called for an ambulance and my daughter Susan to come round. I tried June as well, but I couldn't get hold of her. She was working as a court usher in the Royal Courts of Justice at the time, so had to have her phone off when she was at work.

When the two ambulance men arrived they told Charlie they had to take him into hospital, but for some reason this time he was having none of it. He was shouting, 'You ain't taking me away! I'm not going!' and telling them to F off and all that.

They spent a good half-hour trying to talk him round, and eventually they said to me, 'Look, we can't do nothing, Mrs Brooker, and we really need to hurry up. But could you perhaps try and have a talk with him, as you know he is very poorly, don't you?'

'I know,' I said, getting frustrated. 'What do you think I phoned you up for?'

But anyhow, I was trying all sorts of ways to persuade him, joking with him about it, telling it to him straight, everything. And Susan said to him, 'Look, Dad, we'll come with you, and you will be out before you know it.'

And he just turned round and said, 'If I go in this time, I'm not coming back out.' It was like he knew something was different this time.

We told him to stop being silly, and the driver said to him, 'What's the matter with you, Charlie? We've picked you up before, and then brought you home later, haven't we?'

Finally, he turned to the driver and said, 'All right then, but if I don't fucking well come out, God help you!'

So that was it. At last we went to the hospital. We tried phoning the other kids, and Little Charlie, who was working doing deliveries for a printing and stationery firm, managed to speak to his guvnor and get out of work, so he joined us at the hospital later that morning.

We could tell something wasn't right. He wasn't his usual self, and when me and Susan went to get a coffee, Little Charlie said his dad had been convinced Susan was still in the room, as though he was hallucinating. We stayed with him all day, and they did all sorts of tests on things like his blood pressure and oxygen levels, which were really low.

Then the doctor pulled us to one side and said, 'Charlie is really ill. You know this is probably it now. And I have to say, if anything does happen to him, we don't think it would be in his best interest to bring him back around.'

That was awful. I didn't even want to think that my Charlie mightn't be around, but I knew we had to be prepared for the worst and get the rest of the family down there.

So we called round everyone, and Stephen and Lynne got down there, as well as some of the grand-children. Carol was away on holiday with Mark and the kids in Spain, though, and June was at a concert in Central London as it was her birthday and all the kids had bought her a ticket to see The Who. She hadn't wanted to go, but we had told her she should and that everything would be fine.

Charlie wasn't daft – he knew what was happening. And there was one moment I remember when he squeezed my hand and said, 'Tata, girl.' I couldn't take it and just shook my head and told him to shhh.

Eventually, around 10 p.m., we decided to go home to sleep. By then we were feeling a bit happier 'cause the doctor had got him to wear this big mask that he said would bring his oxygen levels up. And true enough, soon after he started wearing it his levels began to improve.

So we all left except Stephen, who stayed talking to him about this and that for another hour or so. But after he left, the doctors told us that Charlie called them over and asked them to take the mask off. They tried to persuade him, but they couldn't go against what he wanted. That makes me so sad, but I think he knew it was his time. He just knew.

Meantime, we were all at our homes sleeping. It was about 2 or 2.30 a.m. when the phone went and we were told to get back to the hospital quickly. After he had taken the mask off his levels had gone down and down. But we didn't make it back in time. Charlie had died. 28 June 2007 it was. That's a date I'll never forget.

Carol and her family flew back home the next day. And do you know what? Like a cruel twist of fate, the NHS phoned Carol that day and told her they had an appointment for Charlie's feet come free, and they would come to him this time. 'Well,' she told them, 'you are too late. He is dead.'

It was horrible without Charlie around and I felt completely lost. I was just so totally devastated. And I thought to myself, 'That's it now, what's the good of me? I've got nothing else to live for.' The house was strange and empty, and I just couldn't get my head around the fact that Charlie was never coming back. I moved around in a kind of fog, too numb to cry most of the time. But we pushed on with the funeral plans, and held it a week later on the Friday.

The night before the funeral the girls decided that the three of them should stay over with me, so we sat up late into the evening talking and exchanging memories. It was actually a real laugh. I didn't want to sleep in Charlie's bed, 'cause it seemed wrong somehow, and then the girls started being the same. So we were all packed in to my one like sardines!

But the funny thing is, I can sleep on a line. I don't stop all day, but the minute my head hits the pillow, that's it, I'm out. It used to drive Charlie mad – he'd be lying there awake, annoyed I'd fallen asleep so quick, and he'd poke me and say, 'How can you be asleep already? Wake up!'

But Carol is the same as me, and even though it was the night before the funeral, the two of us were straight out. June and Susan stayed awake the whole night, though, and the next day said they couldn't believe how we had done it! They had ended up getting up and making cups of tea and chatting, but me and Carol missed all of that.

The funeral was held at Forest Park Crematorium in Hainault. There were quite a lot of people there as he was so well known. The two boys, Stephen and Charlie, carried the coffin in along with the three girls' husbands, Del, John and Mark, and my niece's husband, which was nice. But the actual funeral passed in a bit of a blur for me. I remember Stephen doing a speech, along with a couple of the grandkids, Danielle and Mark, I think, but mostly we were too upset to speak.

Afterwards we all went back to the house in Dagenham. We'd had a marquee put up in the back garden and everyone met there. It was such a sad day, but you can't sit there moaning – and that's not what Charlie would have wanted. So everyone had their cry, and then everyone had a good time. It was lovely in the end.

Charlie's body was cremated, so I got his ashes put into pots. I gave one to each of the kids, and kept one myself. I like having part of Charlie so close to me, and I often wonder if he is still here. Sometimes I wonder if he is listening while I'm talking about everything in this book, and wanting to cut in and correct me or make a joke! I like to think so, and in a way he is still around, as he is so alive in my memories and always will be.

TWENTY

Lost and Alone

I didn't know what to do with myself once I didn't have Charlie to look after any more. I thought I was just really there to live out my life until it was over. I thought I was finished. I would wake up in the morning and not know what to do with myself. I'd think, 'What am I doing sitting here?' Normally I'd have been up and washing or ironing, and making use of every spare five minutes I had to do things. But I just thought, 'What's the point?' Without my Charlie to do it for, there seemed no reason. It all felt pointless.

Much as there were times when Charlie was alive when I wished for a bit of peace, or I got tired of hearing, 'Pat, I need so and so. Can you sort that for me?' But once it wasn't happening, I missed it and felt lost without it.

And, of course, I cried. How could I not have? But

I was not one for sitting and sobbing my heart out, 'specially if there were people around. I don't like others to see me being too emotional, 'specially my family – it's not good. Yes, I'd shed a tear in front of them, but they were never going to see me completely break down in front of them.

I was frightened in the house on my own too. Charlie had always made me feel really safe, even when he wasn't physically fit. There was something about having him around that made me feel protected. But after he had gone I hated to be home alone.

I started to keep the truncheon in my bedside table that he had carried in his special trouser pocket in The Rising Sun. He had kept it by our bed in case any thief had chanced their luck in the night. I always used to tell him he couldn't use it in case he seriously damaged, or even killed, someone. But he'd laugh and tell me, 'Anyone breaks in here, this is my property and I will defend it – I will give it to them proper!'

Well, the boys used to tell me that I should still remember that was there, and if I got frightened, I could use that against anyone breaking in. But I never would have, in case I ended up killing someone and going to prison! I know I'm not strong, but still, you never know . . .

So instead we got the house all alarmed up, and the

271

boys gave me this great big round yellow torch. If I wasn't going to bash the burglar, they told me, at least I could blind them! But that got daft. I was so jumpy in that first while on my own that I kept it by my bedside, and every time I heard the littlest noise – say, the boiler heating up – I'd grab the torch and turn it on, shooting this beam into the darkness. But there never was anyone there, and the only person who ever got blinded was me!

They also got me a mobile phone, which I had no use for at all in the beginning, but over time I have actually become quite attached to it. Though there is still no point in expecting me to text – just pick up the phone and call, for goodness' sake!

One thing I did realize was that I had completely relied on Charlie financially. Yes, I looked after him twenty-four hours a day, but in many other ways he had looked after me. He was the one who had always sorted out the money, working out what we would buy and what we had left to spend, and he had created this stable home life for us. And suddenly I had no one to tell me what to do with money.

It sounds daft that at seventy-one years old I was out of my depth with money, but it was true. He had always taught me to be careful with it, yes, and I had become more aware of what we were spending once the kids left home, but I had never had it in my hands to decide what to do with it.

One of the things I noticed my children did was to start encouraging me to spend it. It was like I never knew I was allowed stuff, but they got me to start buying clothes and treating myself. I had never had my nails done, so they encouraged me to do that, and to do things for myself just because I wanted to and I could.

It was a strange feeling – even now I feel like I am spoiling myself in a way, and it feels daft. But I do enjoy being able to do what I want now. I know my kids were trying to change my life, and in a way they did. Then the girls started encouraging me to go and stay with them. Susan and Carol didn't work full time, so it was easy for me to go and spend a few days with them, and it was nice too.

And then sometimes I'll look after the children if the girls want to go away – although some of the places, I don't know . . . Carol wanted to go off to boot camp once, so I looked after her youngest daughter. But a boot camp to get fit? Whoever heard of something so ridiculous!

I said to her, 'If you think you have put on weight, just run up and down the stairs twenty times a day! Or take on a bit of the stress I have . . .' Please, give me strength. Honestly, these daft things people get caught up in these days.

Everyone has a different pace of life and set of priorities now, though. Like when I see my kids not eating proper food because they have been too busy to cook, and I think why didn't you plan ahead last night if you knew you would be busy today? Cut up some meat and veg and make a stew the night before, and all you have to do is heat it up the next evening. But that's not how things work now, I see that.

Though sometimes the roles reverse, and they now tell me off! Say, like I will still have the odd cigarette, although never in my house. But I'll stand at the back door, and when they come round they start sniffing, 'Have you been smoking, Mother?'

'No, I have not!'

'You have!'

'Yeah? Well, I need one to calm my nerves. We are all allowed a vice, and you all like your wine or spirits, and I don't do none of that, so let me be with my cigarettes.'

And they laugh at me, but right enough, they do leave me alone!

Through it all, I have moments of hoping that Charlie is still there, keeping an eye on things. There was one day when I had the sliding door open in my lounge, which led out to the back garden. I came downstairs and saw something in the room, and thought it must be a cat had come in. But then I looked again and heard cooing and realized it was a bird, just sitting there looking at me. It was an enormous big thing, like a proper wood pigeon.

Well, I crept round so as not to frighten it, and pulled the curtain up to try and encourage it out the door. You should have seen the performance I was going through! But it turned round and had a look at me for ages, before it finally left. It shook me up a bit, but I forgot about it until the next week.

One of the kids had encouraged me to go along and see a psychic. I thought it was all a bit daft, but I went anyway. But one of the first things she said to me was, 'Your husband came back and visited you.'

That upset me a bit, and I said, 'Oh, stop it, please.'

But she carried on, 'You've had a visitor, haven't you? It was a flying animal.'

Course then I started crying, and tried to tell her about the pigeon.

'Yes,' she said, 'and wherever you go, that bird will be there'.

And do you know what? Whenever I go round Carol's there is always one sitting on the wall. If I go to Susan's, there is always one sitting on her fence. A big, grey thing, just sitting there looking at me. And although I haven't the foggiest if it is the same bird, or Charlie for that matter, there is a bit of me that likes the idea. I'm sure it's a load of ol' nonsense, but I don't suppose there is any harm in liking that pigeon all the same.

A year after Charlie died, life continued on in its funny circles, with a death and a baby one after the other.

The only close family I now had left other than my children was my brother Tommy. We had always got on well, although we had never been close, I think because we had quite different lives. Whereas my house was always the hub of social activity, he and his wife were more private people. Going to the pub and drinking and being at the centre of every party was not his thing, while that had always been Charlie's way, and my dad's. So although we got on well when we did meet up, and he was a genuinely lovely man, we probably didn't get together as often as we should have.

As Charlie had now died, and my dad had passed away a few years before, I reassured myself that, well, at least I still had Tommy. And he was as fit as a fiddle and always very healthy, so I imagined he would be around for years to come. But a year after I said goodbye to my husband, I had to do the same with my brother. I came home from a cruise with Carol to a phone call from his wife, saying he had died of a sudden heart attack.

They had waited for me to come home to tell me, and were burying him in three days' time. Oh, that was a real shock that was. I was just glad I had five amazing kids around me.

Then at the same time my granddaughter Kelly, who had been trying for a long time to fall pregnant, had a baby. My husband was always willing for it to happen for her, but it never did. Well, shortly after he died, she did get pregnant, and she said to me, 'Nan, please God this is going to be a little boy. I want a little Charlie.' And, sure enough, she gave birth to a baby boy, with a shock of ginger hair, and named him Charlie. That's the thing about life – it goes round and round in a never-ending cycle, and for every bad thing, there's always something good just waiting to happen.

Carol's son Mark was friends with a lad called Jack Tweed, who was the same age as him. They had met when they were eight years old, when they both went to St John's School in Buckhurst Hill. I knew him a bit, from him coming around when I was over at their house. Then one day Mark told us that Jack had started dating a girl off the television – Jade Goody. She had been on a series of *Big Brother* and had made quite an impression, so by association Jack suddenly became a celebrity as well. It was quite strange to watch.

I remember Carol once ringing me when I was on my way to their house and telling me to hurry up 'cause Jack and Jade were round there and she wanted me to meet her. She was a lovely bubbly girl, as I remember, always smiling and giggling.

But then not long after I met her she was diagnosed with cancer and told she didn't have long to live. It was a horrible affair, with her being so young and all.

Anyway, Jack proposed and they got married, with Mark as the best man. I was invited and went with Carol. It was really moving, and both sad and happy at the same time, if you know what I mean.

Then just a month later we went to her funeral. Absolutely terrible. And her two lovely young boys left without a mother.

It was the first time I had seen celebrity in action, though. The number of newspapers and photographers that followed the pair of them around was crazy. And the way Jack got treated, just because he was dating her was madness. I remember going to Madame Tussauds with Carol and her family and Jack. There was this huge queue, which we joined, but then Jack disappeared, saying he would sort it. Before we knew it, the whole lot of us had skipped the queue – and got in for free! Just because the lady working there knew who he was from the newspapers, we got that kind of treatment. I couldn't believe it. But it wasn't long before it was to be the norm for me and my family too.

Everyone always told Mark that he should be on television. He is a good-looking lad, confident, and gets on easily with lots of people. He had also learned a bit about the whole celebrity world through his friendship with Jack and Jade and, as far as I could see, liked what he saw.

Well, Mark knew this lad called Brian Belo who had been on that reality TV show *Big Brother* and was also from Essex. I think they knew each other from out in clubs and that. And Brian always used to say the same thing to Mark – that he would be great on TV.

From what Mark has told me, Brian wanted to make some kind of TV show. After he had got a taste for television in the *Big Brother* house, he wanted to try his hand at actually producing something, a different kind of reality TV show. And Mark said to him that he should do a version of *The Hills* – which I have never seen, but from what they told me is an American reality show – but they should set it in Essex.

So Brian said he would give it a go, and Mark got some friends together, and they did a DVD of them talking about themselves and life in Essex and what have you, and then Brian sent it off to production companies.

Then what happens next is the bit that gets all

confused, and I don't really know what happened, but I do know that there is a legal argument about it and Brian is now suing. Somewhere along the line a production company called Lime Pictures started casting for a programme they were making that ended up being called *The Only Way Is Essex* – or *TOWIE* for short.

But anyway, as far as I know, this lady called Sarah Dillistone, who ended up being the producer of the first series, interviewed Mark for the producers. She was a lovely lady, who loved Mark to bits, and she was keen to make sure he was on the show. But then he called Carol up one day and said, '*TOWIE* want to meet you and Dad!' Carol immediately said they didn't want to, and there was no way they were being filmed.

Mark had also hit a problem 'cause he had told this Sarah that his family were multimillionaires, as that is what they all are on *The Hills*, apparently, and he thought we had to be the same. But, of course, we ain't – and in fact we didn't have to be for *TOWIE*!

It was crashing down around him, and he was panicking, so he told Carol, 'Mum, you have to go along with meeting them 'cause they are using other families from Essex, and I have got to have my family on it or they are threatening to get rid of me.'

So Carol agreed that her and her husband Mark would do a little bit of filming in his kitchen – not that his dad, Big Mark, was happy about it! But I think that all went fine.

And then someone from Lime met my granddaughter, Mark's sister Jessica, and loved her. But when they had been talking to her, apparently she had gone on about me quite a bit, and 'cause Mark had talked about me too, they decided they needed to see me!

But Carol told Mark that he couldn't do that to me. Apparently she said to him that I wasn't a glamorous Essex granny, and she was sure that is what they would be after. That I am just a normal old lady and that's not what they would want! Now, a lot of this I didn't know at the time as I think they were keeping it from me – but I found out later!

Well, the show still hadn't even been aired – this was all for a pilot – but I agreed to go along and meet them, just to help Mark out really, to make sure he got his role.

So I met with some people from Lime working on the show and sat there talking with 'em about real life. I can't remember exactly what, just everyday things, like what I did from day to day and my family, and what I thought of Essex and all that. That was all really – I was just ordinary, being myself like. I wasn't being interviewed or anything. And afterwards Sarah Dillistone phoned up Carol and went, 'We love Nanny Pat! we want her on the show!'

Poor Carol was like, 'Oh no, Mum! What are you going to do?!'

But I agreed to do it because in the beginning I thought it was only going to be a one-off appearance, and I thought to myself, 'Why not? It'll be a bit of a laugh and give me something different to do.'

The funniest thing was that, had Charlie still been alive, he would have loved to have been on *TOWIE*! Like I've said, he loved being the centre of attention, and singing, and acting, and dressing up. He was a very loud, funny, entertaining man. So at that moment, he must have been looking down on me, feeling very, very jealous, saying, 'How dare you? You've taken my role!'

So then I had to go along and do this bit of filming. And while I thought the whole thing was totally daft, and I wasn't all that fussed about it, I was nervous too. I had no idea what to expect or what I was supposed to be doing really.

Susan took me along to Mark's flat the first time and I remember saying to her before I went in, 'I'm only doing the one bit for this show, I tell ya.'

Now, the thing with *TOWIE* is it is a reality show, but it is also a bit manipulated, partly for ease of filming, but partly to give people something interesting to watch. So what they wanted me to do was something I often do for my kids and grandkids anyway – drop off some food for him. Why they thought that would be interesting I have no idea, but I agreed to do it with the cameras there. It was weird 'cause I was told just to do what I would do normally, say what I would normally say to Mark, and react to anything just as I would usually. So I wasn't acting, but it's still funny watching it back. I don't sound quite like me – you can tell the cameras were making me feel strange! I think there were three cameras in the room, which is generally how many they have.

Well, I remember coming back out to Susan's car after, where she was waiting, and I was like, 'Never again! No more. I'm not doing no more.'

The whole thing had just felt too daft to me, and too much of a different world to what I was used to – despite it being my real life that they were filming, if you know what I mean!

283

TWENTY-ONE

The Bright Lights of Essex

Well, my great plans to do just the one cameo appearance wasn't the way it worked out. Because, for whatever reason, when the first series was aired on ITV2 in October 2010 apparently the viewers loved my scene, and so did producers. And I got told that Facebook and Twitter, or whatever those Internet sites are called, went crazy with people talking about me! I'll be honest, I still can't see why, but I'm not going to complain. So before I knew it, I was filming again, this time doing a similar thing, but dropping off a sausage plait.

And that seemed to go down even better! I never have understood why my sausage plait has gathered such cult fame, but this was the beginning of it. Bit by bit I began filming more and more scenes, everything from taking a cheese hedgehog to a shop launch with a pig – don't ask – to dressing as the Queen for a fancy-dress party. As I got used to it, I found it more fun. All I was doing was spending time with my family – with a few camera crew there too!

A lot of my role in the first series – and, in fact, the second and third – revolved around Mark's relationship with his on/off girlfriend Lauren Goodger. Now, those two had been together and split up more times than anyone could ever count, ever since Mark was about fourteen years old. And while I wish the girl well, she isn't the right person for Mark.

As for the rest of the cast, I mostly get on well with them. Arg is one of my favourites – I knew him before through Mark as they are good friends – and we have good banter, but I don't half want to shake him when it comes to the ladies! I've always tried to give him advice and tell him where he's going wrong, first with his ex-girlfriend Lydia and then with his recent ex Gemma, but he don't take no notice. It goes in one ear and out the other, and he really doesn't know how to treat them.

Anyway, all of a sudden there were all these people wanting my signature or asking me for photographs in the street, and newspapers and magazines ringing up to see if they could do an interview. With me! I couldn't believe it. What could I possibly have to say that they wanted to hear?

Lots of people started to tell me I had to take on an agent, so two months after the show first went out, I had a meeting with Emma Rouse, who works at a company called Money Management. She seemed like a nice girl, full of ideas for how I could make the most of my new fame, so we started working together and have stayed together ever since. It still makes me laugh that I have an agent, though!

And I tell you, I am probably more aware of my appearance than I ever have been in my whole life. Hark at me! I'm putting in the most effort now I'm in my seventies!

But it's strange 'cause you suddenly have people criticizing your appearance. And while I'm not one of the youngsters on the show, you still can't help but take it to heart. I remember someone got in touch with ITV2 and said, 'Can you please tell Nanny Pat not to keep wearing black.'

'Well, what's it to do with you?' I thought. 'Mind your own business!'

And, yes, I do normally wear black, but I still thought it was a cheek. But all the same, without even realizing, I suppose I started to wear it less.

As for new clothes . . . well, I've always said that I buy new clothes whenever I need them, but they aren't something I treat myself to just for the sake of it. I can't understand that idea of spending on a top to just wear it once. I might not be as strict as we were during World War II – make do and mend for the sake of your country like, and all that business – but I will repair something if it gets a tear, or sew a button back on rather than getting something brand new.

Anyway, lots of the cast started getting their clothes and shoes for free. Big labels would be sending clothes over for them, but not for me. I carried on buying my clothes for myself. I didn't expect any different, to be honest. But people always reckon I get things for free, and my friends will go to me, 'Oh, I bet that's a freebie you are wearing there,' and I'm like, 'No, honest, I had to pay for it,' but no one believes me. Ah well!

I've lost weight since being on the show too, though it hasn't been on purpose. And no, before you ask, it is not to compete with the amazing figures of all the young *TOWIE* girls! I don't know that it is 'cause I am constantly active 'cause I always have been, but I reckon it's more likely to have something to do with me not having time to eat sometimes!

I would say I was a size 12 when *TOWIE* started, but now I am an 8. You can see it in my hands too. My first wedding ring, which I wear on my right hand, was originally on my fourth finger, but now I have to wear it on my middle finger to stop it from falling off.

I had my hair restyled a bit too, and now get it done at the hairdresser's again regular like. And then there are my teeth. It seems everyone likes to discuss them 'cause I have false teeth. During series four one of my teeth broke when I was in Spain on holiday and I had to get a new set. Well, they are especially neat and white and shiny, and they got talked about on the show, which was rightly embarrassing. And then for a while after, that is what people in the street wanted to discuss more than anything else. They'd stop me and go, 'Let's have a look at your teeth,' and I'd cover them up with my hand and be like, 'Oh, don't . . . I forgot about them!'

I started getting invited to all these events too – the opening of this or that, film premieres, theatre opening nights. It was great! All these things that I had never been able to do before. It was like a door had opened for me, giving me access to things that had been out of my reach my whole life. I became part of a world I never dreamed I'd even get to glimpse inside. And once you are there, everyone wants to give you everything for free – drinks, food, goody bags . . . Although I still don't drink much, mostly just a shandy. Three shandies and I'm drunk! I never say no to the odd glass of champagne, though . . .

Soon, everywhere I went people started recognizing me. I was – and still am – forever hearing whispers of,

'It's Nanny Pat!' or 'Go and ask her to make us a sausage plait!' and all that.

If there is one thing people say to me more than anything, though, it's, 'Oh, ain't you little?' Oh, go away, people! I know I'm tiny! I was five foot when I was younger, but over recent years I have developed arthritis in my spine which makes my back curve over. I think of it kind of like my bones are crinkling up. I've got it in other bits of me as well – my knuckles are developing it, and sometimes it gets so bad I lose all feeling in my hands or I can't pick things up. Other times it aches so badly I have to go to bed with gloves on to try and get a bit of relief.

The one positive thing arthritis has given me, though, is the ability to predict the weather! I remember years ago when I lived with my mother-in-law, she'd walk in and go to me, 'Oh, we're going to get some rain tonight, girl.' And I'd think to myself, 'For God's sake, shut up!' I'd only say that in my head, mind! And me and whoever else was in the room at the time – 'cause everyone else was just as cynical about what she was saying – would go, 'Oh, really? Right, rain tonight is it?' in a way that kind of mocked her, without her realizing.

She always said she had one joint that let her know the weather – her knee, her ankle, her wrist . . . But you know what? I take back them words that I laughed at her for, because it's bloody true! As soon as it is about to start raining, my back starts hurting, my knees get all achey . . . It's like when they say that the cold and the damp gets into your bones, it is actually true.

But anyway, I am getting side-tracked. Back to my fans! I really like meeting them. It's nice to have people be so friendly and interested, and mostly people are really lovely. The only time I don't like it is if I am out for a meal, and it seems like people wait until your food has just arrived before they come over and ask for a picture.

I've asked before if they can wait until I have finished eating, but sometimes people are like, 'Well no, not really, I have to go soon,' and get all impatient like they are owed it. I don't understand that. If I saw a celebrity (it still feels funny saying that about me!), I'd probably be too afraid to go over, but if I did, I would definitely wait until they had finished eating. It's like some people don't have the balance right, and they are too pushy.

Occasionally you also get someone being a bit rude – even if they don't mean it – which can get me down. Like, I remember nipping to a supermarket with my daughter-in-law, Tracey, and she hadn't really seen what it was like for me, being famous. This woman stopped me in there and was all aggressive like. She said, 'What are you doing in a place like this? You must have money, so you should be in a posh supermarket!'

Well, Tracey wouldn't stand for it, and told her we were in there to do our food shopping just like anyone else and she should just leave us alone. The woman felt a bit daft then, I think, and put her head down and walked off. Then a cashier came over and told us to take no notice and that it was nice to have me in there, so it worked out all right in the end.

Then *TOWIE* got nominated for a BAFTA. Oh, that was good news it was. It hardly felt real to be nominated for such a big award and all the main members of the cast were invited to go to the ceremony in May 2011 by Lime.

A few weeks before the big night one of the producers pulled me aside and told me that Debenhams had offered to help me out with an outfit.

Well, I was very happy as I didn't have a clue what I was supposed to wear to a posh do like that. So I went to the shop and a lady helped me pick out a few outfits to try on. I had a lovely day out and in the end I settled on one of the dresses I'd first tried on – this orange dress and a kind of beige jacket and beige shoes and bag to go with it that were lovely. Typical of us women, ain't it? You always go back to the first thing you've tried on after hours of searching!

Anyway, when the actual night arrived I was as nervous as can be! A lot of the cast were going to the awards, which were held at Grosvenor House hotel on Park Lane in London. I went with Carol and when we arrived there were people everywhere – fans, journalists, organizers . . . I felt completely lost. And to get into the awards we had to go down the red carpet! I was completely embarrassed with all the attention and asked if I could just go in through a side entrance! But they said I had to go down the red carpet, and I couldn't get down there quick enough. Even though I felt really good in my new dress, I didn't feel like I should be there alongside celebrities such as Colin Firth and Helena Bonham Carter. Who'd want to talk to little ol' me?!

So I practically ran down the carpet, but I kept getting told off and told to stop and turn around to face this photographer, then turn the other way to face someone else . . . then someone else would be calling out for me and I was sent over to talk to them. I said to the organizers, 'Please get me down here quickly,' as I was so uncomfortable, but they said I had to wait at every cross – they put these crosses on the red carpet to let people know where the best places are to stop for pictures. But there did seem an awful lot of them! And even though I was with Carol, they kept separating us to get our pictures done separately. It was right intimidating, but finally we were able to hurry along and get in there.

As for the actual ceremony, well, *TOWIE* was up for the YouTube Audience Prize – where the public voted for their favourite television show. Everyone kept saying we would win, but we weren't so sure as we were up against *Downton Abbey*, *My Big Fat Gypsy Wedding*, *Sherlock*, *Miranda* and *The Killing*.

But then some lads from a show called *The Inbetweeners* made the announcement, and they said we had won! All the rest of the cast were sat with us, and they jumped up when they mentioned *TOWIE*, but I was in a daze and just sat looking around. I remember someone saying, 'Come on! You've got to get up on the stage!' so I did, and it was amazing to be part of it, I have to say.

I only had one shandy to celebrate after, but it was definitely the occasion. And it is such a great thing to be able to say the show won a BAFTA.

Carol made me laugh about it as well. She always remembers how Charlie told the kids to make sure they looked after me. And she looks up like she is talking to her dad, and says, 'She fucking won a BAFTA! Is that good enough? We've looked after Mummy all right – and now she is earning more money than what you did, Dad!'

Oh, it is really funny how it has all turned around and all come out, innit?!

I've got more confident since then in dealing with the media and going to big events too. You just get used to it. It gets easier the more you practise, I suppose! I did used to be nervous at first, but not now. I'm used to it now.

One thing that's helped me get used to the showbiz life is doing an interview with a different celebrity for *Love It!* magazine every week. They send me to interview everyone from Alex Reid to Tara Palmer Tomkinson, which is quite fun. Everyone had told me before I met Alex, 'Oh, he's horrible. Watch out!' but I actually thought he was quite a nice fella. He was charming and friendly and polite. As for Tara, she was completely crazy, but entertaining. She was about an hour late as she said she had tried to cut her own hair and it had gone a bit wrong. And she brought me a candle from Highgrove that she said Prince Charles wanted me to have, though I have no idea if that is true!

I've been doing it for about a year, and I guess they get me to do the interviews as I probably give a different slant to them. I suppose the things I want to ask are not the same as what other people always ask, and people talk to me differently knowing I am not a journalist.

My favourite out of the people I have interviewed was Peter Andre. He sat there holding my hand the whole way through and kept kissing me, and by the end I was getting a bit embarrassed 'cause it was hot and the sweat was rolling off me as well! I remember thinking, 'Please, I wish you wouldn't keep doing that!' But really, he was a right charmer.

I asked him how his brother was doing as he had been ill, and how his mum and dad were doing, and you know what he said? 'Pat, when they come over to stay, you have to come over and have dinner with us.' And he got his PR to make a note of it. I thought, 'Bleedin' hell, can you believe that? Dinner with Peter Andre and his parents!' So yeah, he was a really lovely fella.

I haven't actually interviewed anyone I didn't like, but some of the younger boys can be a bit naughty. Frankie Cocozza annoyed me with how low he wore his trousers. I was like, 'Pull 'em up, lad. I don't need to see your pants!' and I think he took notice of me as any pictures I have seen of him since there are no pants in sight!

And as for those Jedward boys . . . oh, they didn't half play about and act the goat. They kept on dancing and jumping about, and I told 'em, 'Behave yourselves.' But they carried on and were so full of energy that in the end I snapped, 'For God's sake, sit down, will ya! If you don't, I'll . . .' And then they did sit!

I have been on other TV shows now apart from

TOWIE, like *Family Fortunes*, but I 'specially like *This Morning*. I have done a few things with them and been on for different reasons, although my favourite was showing viewers how to make a sausage plait, and judging ones made by other members of the *TOWIE* cast.

But my most memorable TV moment was probably when I ended up being the queen for *Daybreak* at one point! In the run-up to the diamond jubilee they ran a competition to find Britain's best grandmother, and they got it down to a shortlist of people who I had to go and surprise. I was going all over the country to visit these people who had all done amazing things, from raising their grandkids single handedly, to battling all kinds of diseases and setbacks. But I was always dressed as the Queen and I would be sat in this great big Rolls Royce! And people would be looking in the car while I was sitting ducked down, thinking, 'No, please don't spot me,' 'cause it was supposed to be a surprise when it was aired. But a couple of times people thought I actually was the Queen and started calling out to their friends! I can laugh about it now, but at the time I felt quite stressed out! It was good fun, though, and the woman who won, called Betty, was a really deserving winner.

Sometimes, when I look at all the work I do in a week, it can be crazy. When we are filming *TOWIE* I am on standby for that every day – sometimes I get called in and sometimes not – then I am doing photo shoots and TV shows, as well as *Love It!* interviews. And in between it all I am trying to keep up a normal life – see my family, keep my house clean, do my washing, all that kind of thing. But all in all, if I am honest, I do really enjoy the way my life has gone.

And while I started off my first book, *Penny Sweets and Cobbled Streets*, wondering if Charlie was laughing at me from above for having my moment of fame and going, 'What the bleedin' hell you doing, girl?!' I like to think he has changed his mind now. I really hope he is proud of me – proud that I didn't give up without him, and that, with my family's help and the arrival of *TOWIE*, I've more than just got on with life. I have really lived it.

What I like to think is that maybe, just maybe, he is actually looking down on me with one of his cheeky grins and a twinkle in his eye, going, 'Good on ya, girl.'

RECIPE

Sausage Plait

Since I've got famous, I don't think anyone has asked me any question as much as, 'Go on then, Pat, tell us . . . how do you make a sausage plait?' So here you go! It's pretty straightforward, cheap and tasty, and it's the very same recipe I was taught to do at school all those years ago. I have made this like thousands of times since.

The way I used to do it for me and Charlie was to make one of an evening and eat half of it hot with new potatoes and peas. Then the next day we would have the other half cold with salad. But you can serve it any way you like!

INGREDIENTS:
500g puff pastry; 500g sausage meat
25g butter; 1 egg, beaten
1 small onion, diced

METHOD:

1. Preheat the oven to 170°C/gas mark 3. Roll out the pastry to a 30cm square.

2. Melt butter in a frying pan, add the onion and cook gently for 5–10 minutes, until softened. Leave to cool.

3. Place the sausage mixture along the centre of the pastry, leaving a border of about 4cm empty at the top and bottom. Then spoon the onions evenly over the top of the sausage meat.

4. Cut slits in the pastry from about 3cm away from the sausage mixture to the edge, approximately 2cm apart.

5. Fold either end of the pastry over the sausage meat, then take pastry strips from alternate sides and position them over the sausage meat to make a plait. Tuck any extra strips underneath. Glaze the plait with beaten egg.

6. Transfer to a baking tray and cook for 45–55 minutes, or until golden brown and cooked through.

ACKNOWLEDGEMENTS

Writing this book was great fun, but also hard work, and I had help from lots of lovely people along the way, who I want to thank from the bottom of my heart.

First off, of course, is my family. All my kids, grandkids, even my great grandkids, have been amazingly supportive. We are a close family, and always will be, and it's wonderful to know we always have each other to rely on. So a big thank you to all of them.

To my manager, Emma Rouse from Money Management, whose patience and loyalty to me and my family has been fantastic, and whose hard work has made the last year so much easier. Thank you!

I would also like to thank Emma Donnan, who did a brilliant job of helping me get my memories onto paper.

To Ingrid Connell, Lorraine Green and the rest of

the team at Pan Macmillan for all their hard work on the book. And to Andrew Lownie, for his help in making the book happen in the first place.

And finally to all the staff at ITV and Lime Pictures for looking after me throughout my *TOWIE* journey.

Picture Acknowledgements

All photographs from the author's private collection, apart from page 8, top picture © Dave M Bennett/Getty Images, bottom picture © Piers Allardyce/Rex Features

extracts reading groups
competitions books new
discounts extracts
competitions
books new
events books
extracts
new reading groups
interviews
events extracts
discounts
new books events
events new
discounts extracts discounts

www.panmacmillan.com

extracts events reading groups
competitions books extracts new